CONSPIRACY KILLERS SNARED

Ronald E Bowers

Former Senior Prosecutor
Los Angeles County District Attorney's Office

Some names and locations have been changed to protect the privacy of individuals connected with this story. Certain events have been inferred from the facts of these cases.

Ronald E. Bowers, Publisher
losangelestruecrime@aol.com

ISBN 978-1-7326655-5-2

First release April 2019

INTRODUCTION

In this day and age, the public takes for granted the fact that criminals are caught and prosecuted for their crimes. However, in real life it isn't an automatic process but dependent on the motivation, competency and tenacity of the detective assigned to investigate the crime. In other words, some criminals can get away with Murder if the detective assigned to their case doesn't vigorously do his or her job.

What has amazed me over my 43 years as a prosecutor is the incredible work done by extraordinary detectives. These individuals do their job without fanfare and seldom receive any recognition by the community they serve. I have often wondered what drives these detectives to do such a remarkable job? I can't say there is one characteristic that differentiate the exceptional detective. Some detectives might be motivated by a feeling of righteous indignation that a person who violates the law is able to evade apprehension and punishment for their bad conduct.

Others take their job seriously believing they are trying to make their community safer by taking predatory criminals off the streets. However, there may be less laudatory reasons that induce detectives to go the extra mile. Some detectives approach their jobs as though they are hunting game or fishing and are driven by the 'thrill of the catch.' To them it might be a challenge to try to outsmart the crook. A more basic approach might be the mere fact that the detective just wants to apprehend the 'asshole' for the mere principle of it.

But others attribute it to a more military approach. Some believe that detectives are driven by a feeling that they want to carry on a tradition of excellence for their law enforcement agency. Often a detective will feel a dedication to the agency they work for. Over the years some police departments have gained a reputation for being able to ALWAYS get their crooks. There is an elitist attitude instilled in them from the time they go through the police academy. They possess a certain unique quality to do outstanding work.

Part of that feeling of being a superior police department comes from the public image of a department. LAPD as a department has had the opportunity of being idealized by TV programs. The reason that LAPD garnered so much attention from television and motion picture industry was the fact that it policed the Hollywood area. This attention started way back in the late 1940s with the *Dragnet* radio program by Jack Webb and continued when it was made into one of the earliest TV programs.

A spinoff of *Dragnet* was the popular *Adam 12* TV series showing how officers patrolled the streets of Los Angeles. Fictional characters like Sgt. Friday and Sgt. Colombo have been immortalized in the mind of the public as to how detectives' approach and investigate crimes.

Besides the TV programs, there have been real-life LAPD detectives who have taken on a larger-than-life image. These individuals have created the mold that today's LAPD homicide detectives attempt to emulate.

Before World War II, the Los Angeles Police Department (LAPD) had a jaded reputation for being corrupt and infiltrated by members of organized crime. During this time Hollywood became the center of the motion picture industry. Movie making was a lucrative business which attracted mobster characters from the east coast.

At the time, the most notable mobster was Bugsy Siegel, along with his lieutenant Mickey Cohen. However, there were others from the underworld like Jack Dragna, Jack Whalen and Jimmy Fratianno who were fighting for a part of the action in the sprawling city of Los Angeles. They were able to extort money from the movie studios as well as to take control of the prostitution business and gambling operations. During the 1930s and early 1940s organized crime had extended their tentacles into the police department. The mob had influence over some corrupt police officers who looked the other way when crimes occurred on their police beats. Even at times they were able to infiltrate the police vice detail, giving them control of the gambling and prostitution businesses.

After World War II the city fathers of Los Angeles had enough of the corruption and violence caused by organized crime. The politicians wanted the laws to be enforced especially as they pertained to vice activities. In order to carry out the wishes of the civic leaders it was necessary for the LAPD to make some changes. In 1946 the Chief of Police Clemence Horrall created an Intelligence Division later known as the Gangster Squad. The original detectives spend most of their time conducting surveillance, wiretapping, and pursuing mobsters.

This Gangster Squad was notorious for the phrase **Mulholland Falling**. For a long time, the mobsters thought they were safe because they were smart enough to know that there was no waterfall anywhere near Mulholland Drive. It wasn't until later that the mobsters realized the real meaning of the saying **Mulholland Falling** was that somehow criminals fell off the cliffs along Mulholland Drive. In fact, the Gangster Squad never threw anyone off the steep cliffs on Mulholland Drive.

However, the Gangster Squad didn't discourage the mobsters from thinking that bad things would happen to them if they stayed in LA committing crime.

The detectives on the Gangster Squad became aware of every move of the mobsters. After the early demise of Bugsy Siegal, the Squad set its sights on pursuing Mickey Cohen. Although it took considerable effort, they got Mickey convicted on tax evasion charges that sent him to Alcatraz federal prison.

With Mickey being sent up the river, organized crime seemed to wither away from tinsel town and the City of Angels. The end result was that the Gangster Squad also faded into history. Over the years books and movies have been made about the LAPD Gangster Squad. (The book ***Gangster Squad: Covert Cops, the Mob, and the Battle for Los Angeles*** was written by Paul Lieberman, and the neo-noir movie ***LA Confidential*** and the more recent movie simply titled ***Gangster Squad*** have enhanced the reputation of this LAPD unit.)

The reputation of the Gangster Squad has been boosted or maybe distorted by another famous group of detectives called the Hat Squad. In the 1950s and 1960s there were four detectives in the Robbery Division who became legends in their own right. These detectives stood out in several ways. First off, they were big guys and all over six feet tall. Without a doubt they were imposing figures and to the criminals they appeared to be intimidating. One might say the crooks feared having any contact with the Hat Squad.

But what was most distinctive about this 'fab four' was the fact that they were always adorned with fedora hats with three-inch brims. Of course, in the summer time their fedoras were exchanged for yellow Panama hats. At all times they were fashionably attired in their tailor-made single-breasted suits that cost them two weeks' salary which was costly on a detectives' salary. These guys were impeccably dressed all the way down to their spit-shined shoes.

This unusual group of detectives clearly stood out because of their imposing appearance. They gained a reputation for being tough with criminals but at the same time being very compassionate with the victims. The underworld learned to stay out of sight of Hat Squad.

This so-called Hat Squad was made up of Max Herman Sr., Clarence 'Red' Stromwall, Harold Crowder and Edward Benson. They were all bright and knew how to out-think the crooks. They worked as a team and were a dominant force in cleaning up the corruption in the city. They were such a tightknit group that when the Korean War occurred, they all enlisted together and went on active duty with the 40th Infantry Division. After the war they returned to LAPD and continued working as the Hat Squad.

Your author began working for the District Attorney's Office in the 1960s. I remember seeing these very distinctive detectives with their old Fedoras bring cases into the DA's Office to be filed. Occasionally I would see them in the preliminary hearing courts. These guys were great to work with since they knew what they were doing. They were truly a living legend of LAPD.

The group finally dissolved in the early 1960s when three of them graduated from law school. They retired from their detective job to become attorneys in Los Angeles. Then in the 1970s two of them became Los Angeles County judges.

However, in the 1970s I was assigned a major Bookmaking case in Clarence 'Red' Stromwell's court. During the courtroom breaks he would tell us stories how he and the Hat Squad ran around town chasing the mobsters. I remember him smoking his large Cuban cigar in his court chambers regaling us with anecdotes about the old gangster days. He said, "We played it to the hilt and chasing bandits in those days was fun."

Besides all the legendary groups such as the Gangster Squad and the Hat Squad, there were individual detectives who became legends in their own right. Maybe the most famous was Sgt. John St John, who was better known as 'Jigsaw John.'

He acquired that name for solving a Murder that occurred in Griffith Park where the victim had been dismembered in a jigsaw manner. His ability to piece together seemingly insignificant details made that moniker stick.

Detective St John was definitely from the old school of detectives. He believed in approaching any homicide in a meticulous manner. He grew up in Los Angeles and joined LAPD in 1942, rising to the rank of detective in 1949. During his career he worked on some of the high-profile cases such as the Black Dahlia, the Night Stalker, the Hillside Stranglers, and the Southside Slayer. The one which made him most famous was the Freeway Killer involving William Bonin. As a matter of fact, his tenacious work on the Bonin case resulted in him receiving the LAPD Distinguished Service Medal.

Even though Jigsaw John wore a Fedora hat he wasn't as dapper as the original members of the Hat Squad. Instead of wearing tailor-made suits he sported a disheveled suit with baggy pants and a drab tie. He might be viewed more as a Peter Falk character in the Colombo TV series than one of the dapper detectives of the by-gone era. That was partly due to the fact that when he was a rookie cop, a prisoner struck him with an iron bar causing him to lose sight in one of his eyes.

Jigsaw John definitively wouldn't qualify for the Fashion Police Squad. However, he gained a reputation as a dogged detective who had an uncanny way of remembering minute facts of complex cases. There was no one better at handling serial Murder cases since he had a mind that could somehow compartmentalize all the massive facts. Of the over 1000 homicides he worked on he was able to solve at least two-thirds of them.

He knew the streets of LA like the palm of his hand and didn't need an old Thomas Guide map to find his way around the city. His famous line was "L.A. is my beat, and I'm going to take care of it." He did it longer than any other detective in LAPD history. He retired in 1993 after working for LAPD for over a half century and 43 years as a homicide detective.

He was immortalized in a book entitled ***Jigsaw John*** which became the ***Jigsaw John*** TV series in 1976 by NBC. Few individuals become legends in the middle of their career, especially homicide detectives. All the notoriety didn't seem to change Sgt. St John. I, the author, remember working with Sgt. John on several cases in the 1960 and 1970s. The best way to describe him was that he was 'a no-nonsense' type who you enjoyed working with since he knew what needed to be done.

To me he was just a homicide detective who seemed to have a sixth sense in solving his Murder cases. However, there were many more exceptional LAPD detectives I had the pleasure of working with. As time went on it became clear that certain cases required more attention so LAPD created the infamous Robbery Homicide Division (RHD). Although it combined the robbery cases with the homicide cases, RHD really became the Go-To Place for the complex homicides occurring within the Los Angeles city jurisdiction.

As a result, nowadays RHD receives the high-publicity cases even though most homicides occurring in Los Angeles are handled by the local LAPD divisions. Unfortunately, the public and the media pay little attention to the Murder cases that are handled by the local police stations. Over the years of being involved in hundreds of Murder cases, I have found that some of the local homicide detectives do an amazing job.

No TV series have been made about the run-of-the-mill homicides handled by the local homicide detectives. Seldom are books written about the grassroots homicides. However, my book series titled ***Today's Sherlock Holmes*** is an attempt to shine some light on what has been long ignored by the media. This book ***Conspiracy Killers Snared*** will give you the reader a chance to see what extraordinary investigation is done by detectives at the local level. You, the reader, will be able to learn about some of the most fascinating Murder cases lying below the radar. You will be amazed at how these unheralded detectives catch their murderers.

CONTENTS

Chapter 1 Usual Saturday Night in the San Fernando Valley 1
Chapter 2 Time to Get Away 7
Chapter 3 They Were Now in Another League 23
Chapter 4 Police Respond 27
Chapter 5 The Dicks Arrive 35
Chapter 6 The Godsend Witness Sally Talles 43
Chapter 7- Assessment of What Evidence They Had 49
Chapter 8-Time to Follow Up 55
Chapter 9 –Bingo- We Have Found It 67
Chapter 10- So Many Loose Ends 73
Chapter 11- Pulling Over the Van 79
Chapter 12- What Was Wife's Role? 81
Chapter 13- Maria's Statements Before Arrest 87
Chapter 14 Search Warrant Time 91
Chapter 15 Statements After Arrest 97
Chapter 16-Time for the Ruse 101
Chapter 17- Wilson Sanchez Comes Clean 105
Chapter 18 What Was Oscar Alvarado's Story? 107
Chapter 19 Who Has the Money? 115
Chapter 20-Pablo Opens Up 121
Chapter 21- It's Erik Monroy's Turn to Sing 125
Chapter 22- Time to Make a Deal 129
Chapter 23- What About the Rest? 133
Chapter 24 Other Tough Contract Killings 137
Chapter 25- Immunity and Leniency 143
Chapter 26- Corroboration 151
Chapter 27- Building a Case 155
Chapter 28- Opening Statement 159

Chapter 29-Opening Statement About Crime 169
Chapter 30- Opening Statement Defendants' Stories 173
Chapter 31- Trial 181
Chapter 32 Witness Sally Talles 185
Chapter 33- Erik Monroy Testimony 191
Chapter 34- Pablo Alvarenga Testimony 199
Chapter 35- Detective Kirby as Witness 209
Chapter 36- Other Prosecution Witnesses 219
Chapter 37-Argument- Explaining the LAW 223
Chapter 38- Argument- Explaining the Law of Conspiracy 231
Chapter 39 Argument- Explaining Phone Records 239
Chapter 40- Argument- Cellphone Towers 245
Chapter 41- Argument- Motive, Insurance, & Bank Records 249
Chapter 42- Argument- Defendant Lying to the Police 253
Chapter 43- Summarizing the Evidence, Defense Argument and Rebuttal 261
Chapter 44- Verdict, Other Trials, & Appeals 269
Chapter 45- Critiquing the Investigation 275
Chapter 46- Sherlock Holmes Approach 283

CHAPTER 1 USUAL SATURDAY NIGHT IN THE SAN FERNANDO VALLEY

It was April 9, 2005, on a lazy Saturday night in San Fernando Valley. Three young guys were cruising around in an old Ford van. Their usual interest was looking for teen-age chicks to hit upon and hopefully impress. But this particular evening they had only 'MURDER on their mind.' They didn't project the steely-eyed image of a ruthless hitman. They could better be described as a bunch of losers gliding aimlessly through life. Their moral compass was either broken or needed to be recalibrated. The driver maneuvered the van to a stop next to the curb painted in bright red. This was next to the corner of Arcola and Stagg streets in Sun Valley, an outlying district of the greater City of Los Angeles. The fact that it was illegal to park in this red zone was a mere technicality that didn't cross their minds.

The driver unhurriedly opened the door and leaped out onto the vacant street. Before closing the driver's door, he motioned to his buddy in the passenger seat to slide over to driver's side of the van. The guy who got out skirted around the front of the old van. The headlights illuminated his body that was clothed in a dirty black sweatshirt. As he headed for the curb, he pulled up the hoodie on the back of the sweatshirt. His left hand clutched a cellphone as his right hand pushed a handgun into his front waistband. His head turned from side to side scanning the area for any night owls wandering the streets.

He assured himself that he was alone as his eyes focused on the cellphone. Carefully he punched in a phone number and slowly placed the phone to his ear. He could hear the phone ringing but no one was answering. It was almost midnight and the caller thought maybe he had called the wrong number. Just before the phone was about to go to voice mail, a woman's faint voice could be heard. She seemed to be whispering into the phone. She asked, "Who is this?" That response came as a surprise and the young man didn't know how to answer. Should he say, "I'm the hitman you requested." Or should he make sure that he was talking to the wife of the man he was there to kill?

With a slight hesitancy in his voice he asked if she was a friend of Mr. Alvarado. These seemed to be the magic words since she responded in an excited voice, "You are the guys I have been waiting for." Then he said, "Well we are outside and are ready." Her response was "Okay I will send him out in a minute." She added, "Let me turn on the front door house light so you can see him better." The conversation was terse and to the point. The guy said, "Alright I will be waiting."

Within the next 60 seconds everyone's lives would be forever changed. The wife had hung up her cellphone and walked to the rear bedroom where her husband had dozed off. She went over to him grabbing his shoulder and shaking him. His body jerked awake with his eyes blinking as though he was trying to focus on his wife who was standing in front of him. His first response was, "What's going on? What's happening?" He shook his head wondering what he was supposed to be doing.

His wife spoke tenderly with the most tantalizing voice she could muster up under the dire conditions and stated, "I've got this splitting headache and I don't have any aspirin. Could you go to the drug store to get me something for my headache?" Her husband, Reynaldo Quijano, looked up and replied like an obedient husband would by saying, "Okay, let me get a sweater." He didn't want to question his wife. If she said she needed something it was easier to go do it then debate the matter with her.

One wonders how this apparently 'loving wife' could so easily send her husband out this cool evening to his death. Did she feel like Judas when he betrayed Christ? It takes a strong determined person to be able to utter the words that will lead to that person's demise.

The husband stumbled his way to the kitchen where he started searching for his car keys. Finding them on the counter he grabbed them and turned toward the front door. When he reached for the door handle, he noticed that it was broken on the inside. For over a month he had promised himself to find time to fix that door handle. He thought to himself that he needed to write a note to himself in order to remind him to add that to his 'fix-it list' or as he called it 'his honey-do list.'

When he pulled the door inward to open and stepped outside, he felt the frosty night air brush against his face. Even for Los Angeles, this could be classified as a 'chilly evening' with a slight northern breeze swaying the palm trees lining the street. As he took a deep breath of the evening air, he inhaled a whiff of jet exhaust from the local airport several blocks away. Although he had lived in this house for 10 years, he hadn't completely acclimated to the jet-fuel smell. When there was a northern breeze, it became apparent that they were on the edge of a airport run way.

He walked over to his well-used brown Mercedes which was parked at the curb. Opening the driver's door, he gradually settled into the comfortable driver's seat. His habit was to always leave his car unlocked since he believed he lived in a safe neighborhood. Since he had just gotten home shortly before, the interior of the car was still slightly tepid not requiring him to turn on the car's heater. Even though this was a

Mercedes, it was one of the older models that required a key to start the engine. Inserting the key in the ignition he gave the key a slight turn to the right which caused the engine to come to life.

With several pumps on the accelerator the engine roared loudly. In a robotic act, he grabbed the seat belt with his right hand and pulled it around until the latch click into place. Since he wasn't in any hurry, he sat in the driver's seat relaxed and started musing about his trip to El Salvador in the morning. Reynaldo was looking forward to the trip to his old home country where most of his family still lived. He had fierce cravings for El Salvador. Was it the spicy food or the alluring music that drew him back? He couldn't verbalize his feelings for his home country but all he knew was that he missed it. Now he was starting to feel nostalgic since it was merely hours before he would start on his journey to the familiar streets of San Salvador.

Throughout the entire day, Reynaldo had been reminiscing about growing up with all of his relatives. He missed his homeland and was looking forward to this return visit. His mind was filled with sentimental thoughts and wasn't thinking on what was going on around him. He was totally oblivious to his immediate surroundings. He certainly didn't notice the guy crouched down near a hedge holding a cellphone in his hand.

However, this other guy's eyes were intently fixed on Reynaldo's every move as he sat in his well-used Mercedes. This hitman had only a nanosecond to decide whether this was the man who he had been hired to kill. Reaching into his pants pocket he pulled out a wrinkled photo of the man he was looking for. He glanced at the photo and then turned to intently stare at the driver of the Mercedes.

The lighting was poor and there was no way to know for certain if this was the right person. He could hear the driver accelerate the engine and then the driver put the car into 'Drive.' This was the moment described by the expression 'Do or Die.' The thought of $8,000 in cold cash flashed across the hitman's mind. This was not the time for self-doubts. Almost automatically the guy reached into his waistband and cautiously pulled out a gun. At that moment he leaned forward and started running as fast as his feet would carry him.

His right hand gripped the 9mm Lugar pointing it straight ahead of himself. Like a sprinter racing to the finish line he ran toward the driver's door of the Mercedes. Even though he wasn't 100% sure this was the right guy to kill, he couldn't take a chance of losing out on the $8,000. This seemed to be the right person in that he came out of the house he had been told to go to. To reassure himself he remembered that he was told that the front door light would be on and he could see the porch light beaming brightly.

As the killer came within twenty feet of the car, he started squeezing the trigger. Instantly he saw a muzzle flash light up the darkness as his hand felt a recoil from his gun. All of a sudden, the stillness of the night was broken by a bullet shattered the driver's side window. The car was gradually creeping forward as though it was pulling away from the curb. Reynaldo, the driver, turned this head toward the shooter and had a shocked expression as shards of glass pierced his stunned face.

All the victim could see was the figure of a person wearing a hoodie running toward his car from across the street. Reynaldo automatically took his foot off of the accelerator and stomped on the brake. Before he could turn his head away, he heard what sounded like a loud fire-cracker noise. As the bullets found their mark in his body, he felt an intense pain to his head.

The car continued to roll forward at a snail's pace as the shooter got to within three feet of the driver's door. This time the shooter pointed the barrel of the gun in a downward angle and fired again. Originally the driver's hands seemed welded to the steering wheel but eventually his grip relaxed. As Reynaldo was trying to assess what was happening to him, he sensed a sharp pain behind his eyes as everything went blank. His eyes froze wide open seeing nothing. His head slumped to the side and fell back against the car's head-rest. Not another thought was being formed in his mind as he entered the state of being 'brain dead.' Without any further thought by Reynold, his body began the deliberate process of drifting into rigor mortis.

CHAPTER 2 TIME TO GET AWAY

Now the shooter had to make a split-second decision. How could he know for certain that he had been triumphant in killing the victim? At the same time, he wanted to get away so he wouldn't be caught. As the shooter gazed at the driver, he observed the driver's clothes turn bloody red. He could infer from that sight that the victim was 'DEAD as a doorknob'. He surely was tempted to shout out to the world 'Mission Accomplished.'

At that moment he spun around on his heels. Then he turned toward the van which was waiting for him. By this time the van had inched into the intersection. His cohorts in the van were more interested in getting away then checking out the status of the victim.

As the shooter approached the van, he opened the passenger door and leaped in. As he slammed the door shut, the driver stomped on the gas making the van lurch forward. Instantly the driver made a left-hand turn and headed down Stagg Street which led to the entrance to the Interstate 5 Freeway. None of the occupants of the van said a word. The only sound was the roar of the van's engine as well as the heavy breathing of the shooter. After a moment of silence, the shooter turned his head toward the driver and spoke in a frightened voice, "Let's get out of here."

The shooters eyes were wide open like saucers. He was 20 years old and went by the name of Wilson Sanchez.

He seemed frozen in the passenger seat. However, as the van reached the freeway on-ramp, he turned to his cohort in the rear seat and handed him the gun. He instructed him to hide the gun in the special place in the rear of the van. His buddy leaned forward and gripped the gun. After the van pulled onto the freeway this guy got up and moved to the rear seat where he stuck the gun into a small compartment under one of the side windows of the van.

This guy in the back was Pablo Alvarenga, 19 years old, whose moniker was 'Basic.'

That title fit his personality in that he was a basic type guy with no outstanding characteristics. His participation in the Murder was limited to being the one who supplied the hoodie sweatshirt that the shooter wore. His only other involvement was that he test-fired the 9mm Lugar to make sure it was operable.

The guy doing the driving was Erik Monroy who was also 19 years old. His main qualification was the fact he was the only one who had a valid driver's license.

The van he was driving was not his but was the shooter's who had his driver's license suspended. The shooter didn't want to be doing anything illegal like driving the van without a valid driver's license (although he had driven out to the victim's house on this second attempt).

The van sped south on the Interstate better known as the Golden State Freeway, after passing over the 134 Freeway interchange approaching the gigantic Griffith Park on its right. This is the City of Los Angeles' answer to the City of New York's Central Park. Some Angelenos will claim that Griffith Park has more spectacular attractions then Central Park. If our hitmen glanced over to the right, they would see the section of the Park called Travel Town with all the old steam locomotives that had thundered across the country during a bygone era. Many of the local kids have vivid memories climbing on these antiquated trains with their old steel railroad cars.

But the most unforgettable place in Griffith Park for any kid is the Los Angeles Zoo which is home for so many exotic animals. However, in recent years the Zoo has become the subject of heated criticism for keeping wild animals in caged conditions.

The Asian Elephant exhibit still existed at the zoo but not without great controversy from certain animal groups. One animal rights group convinced a judge to rule that the pachyderms must have two hours of exercise a day and that the soil of their enclosure be tilled regularly to avoid health issues. The judge went on to say that the Zoo's elephant exhibit is not a happy place and elephants are not able to thrive, be happy or be content.

Somehow these three hitmen zipped passed the Zoo without recalling any fond memories of visiting it. It was doubtful that any of these hitmen had participated in any of the animal rights protests. However they might want to keep in touch with that animal-loving judge if they ever have complaints about prison conditions and the size of their cells.

Since the freeway forms the east border of Griffith Park the hitmen continued past the all-time favorite section for young children which is the old-fashioned Merry-Go-Round ride in Griffith Park. It is one of the hidden jewels that most people miss. It was built in 1926 and installed in the park in 1937. What makes it unique is that it has 68 jumper horses carved out of wood. What makes them a kid's favorite is their colorful painting as well as the sounds from the Stinson 165 Military Band Organ which vibrates out music from previous eras when life was slower and friendlier.

Each one of these occupants of the van seemed fixated on receiving the money for the killing job. Wilson Sanchez had actually seen the $8,000 in cold hard cash. He vividly remembered the stack of hundred-dollar bills mixed with some twenty-dollar bills. None of the guys were concerned about all the cultural features of Griffith Park. What they did have in common with the founder of the park was that they all had been involved in the shooting of another human being.

Griffith J. Griffith had gained a fortune through mining operations and was able to acquire a major portion of the Rancho Los Feliz. In the 1890s he donated over 3000 acres of his vast estate to the City of Los Angeles. Because of his generosity the city named the park after him. However, by 1903 circumstances changed after he had been convicted for shooting and severely wounding his wife. When he was released from prison he offered to pay for a new amphitheater, observatory, and planetarium in order to curry favor for himself with the city fathers. It was a tough call for the city politicians, who turned done his offer; however, later the city accepted his donation for the building of the Greek Theater and Griffith Observatory.

Most likely our hitmen weren't that familiar with Griffith's criminal behavior. But they could have learned something about how money can try to buy back your reputation. As the old dilapidated van rolled along the Golden State freeway the guys surely glanced to the left to see the concrete monolith making up the Los Angeles River. What controversy could swirl around one of the great engineering marvels for Los Angeles. For years there had been devastating floods through the El Pueblo de Los Angeles. Finally, the civic leaders were able to convince the U.S. Army Corp of Engineers to encase the river's bed and banks in concrete providing for a wide flood-control channel through the city.

Since its building in 1938, this great concrete canal has protected the city from flooding. However, today a group called the Friends of the Los Angeles River is advocating for habitat restoration and public access to the LA River. Their desire is to have the US Army Corps of Engineers spend a half a billion dollars to restore nearly 600 acres of the river to a wildlife habitat. That means tearing out the concrete bottom and walls. They want to have a running body of water for recreational use. However, for most of the year the water would have to be provided from the Tillman Water

Reclamation Plant which obtains its water from the sewage from some 800,000 homes.

Not one of the hitmen had wasted any of their brain cells contemplating whether they wanted to kayak down through the new wildlife habitat section of the LA River supplied by reclaimed sewer water.

As the buddies continued down the Golden State Freeway, the driver of the van was concentrating on his driving skills since he didn't want to be pulled over by the police after doing a hit, especially since they still had the gun in the car. The driver had his eyes glued to the speedometer to make sure that he didn't exceed the 65-speed limit on the freeway. This required him to drive in the right-hand lane with the other cars zipping by them on their left. It wasn't hard for the driver to stay under the 65 mile per hour since the aged Ford van was on its last legs and had difficulty even maintaining the basic speed limit.

As they reached the Arroyo Seco Parkway they exited the Golden State Freeway and made the sharp right onto what is the first freeway in the Western USA. Almost instantly they came upon a huge freeway sign for the Stadium Way turnoff, and the van started to pick up speed on the downward slope approaching downtown. The guys looked to the right seeing the entrance to the **Los Angeles Dodgers Stadium**.

The stadium was built back in 1962 causing a tsunami of controversy. The original site of the stadium was called Chavez Ravine where the poor Spanish-speaking residents lived. The city used the power of eminent domain to force those residents to move out. Ultimately the baseball stadium was built on top of all the razed homes. When it was completed it became the world's largest baseball stadium, with a seating capacity of 56,000. It is considered a Pitcher's ballpark since there have been 12 no-hitters in this stadium.

The hitmen weren't concerned about all the hullabaloo in building the stadium but they were more concerned about the performance of their favorite Dodger players. That evening the Dodgers had not played at home but were in Arizona where the D'Backs beat them 5 to 4. These hitmen were lamenting that the Dodgers had lost and blamed it on the poor pitching. It seemed strange that these guys had constructive comments about a professional baseball team whose games they had never attended.

As the van cruised down the Elysian hill, they could barely make out the Los Angeles City Hall to their left. It was built in 1928 to a height of 453 (32 floors), which was the tallest building that could be built in the city up until 1964.

It took years for engineers to convince the city that new types of construction made it safe to build taller buildings. The city hall structure is so identifiable because of its unique tower which is in the shape of the Mausoleum Mausolus located in Bodrum, Turkey and was one of the Seven Wonders of the Ancient World. However, the locals call the structure the 'Pointy' building.

When the guys viewed the City Hall they weren't thinking about the Ancient Wonders of the World. They felt a sigh of relief since they were now back on their own turf.

They had no problem zipping through the famous four-level freeway interchange. It had been built back in 1949 with the cloverleaf design when freeway travel was thought to be innovative. The idea of ribbons of concrete roads with no stop signs was a concept foreign to old-time motorists. The original concept of the interchange was that motorists could travel at high speed without having to stop for cross traffic. However, nowadays this famous interchange at rush hour is nothing but a curvy parking lot.

Since it was after midnight, the guys were able to whizz through the interchange without any delay. The Los Angeles streets are designated by numbers starting from the city hall which is located on First Street. Since the guys had passed the city hall, they knew they were only 81 blocks or streets from being back home. At that point, the freeway is called the Harbor Freeway weaving through the high-rise buildings making up the downtown business district of LA.

At the south end of the downtown area, they could see the lit-up Staples Center where these guys took pride in the winning record of the Los Angeles Lakers. One of the guys bragged to the two others that he still had his Number 32 jersey of superstar player Coby Bryant. Now that he would soon be $8,000 richer, he was contemplating that he would be able to afford to attend more future Laker home games. The shooter, Wilson Sanchez, couldn't help himself from feeling a little giddy. He was like a kid at Christmas time who had just received a bunch of gift cards and started anticipating all the items he could now afford to buy.

By then they were passing the USC campus on the west side of the Harbor Freeway. None of the guys in the van had ever contemplated enrolling at this prestigious university.

The yearly tuition was more than any of their family members earned in an entire year. However, all of them were avid USC football fans. As they glanced to the west next to the sprawling campus, they could see the outline of the infamous LA Coliseum.

This structure was built in 1923 as a memorial to LA veterans of WWI. The USC football team played their home games there. However, when the Olympics were planned for 1932, the stadium was increased in size to hold seating for 101,574. Later in 1984 the Olympics were held in the stadiums again and the seating capacity has been reduced to 78,500.

Many USC athletes have played on this gridiron. None of the hitmen remembered any of the great football players such as Mike Garett, Charles White and Marcus Allen. They had a slight recollection that some guy named O.J. Simpson had played in the Coliseum for USC. All they could recall was that he had won the Heisman Trophy but later got into some type of trouble killing some people. None of these neophyte hitmen seemed to consider that they were in the same killing league as O.J. Simpson.

By then they were coasting down the freeway off-ramp onto Manchester Boulevard. After a few turns they pulled over at Pablo's place.

Pablo had told Wilson that he would keep the handgun in his apartment until they could return it to its rightful owner. Pablo, who was seated in the back, went over to the hiding compartment of the van and removed the handgun. He cradled it in his hands as though this piece of steel was some type of sacred object that they all revered.

Carefully Pablo inserted the gun in his waistband and covered the handle with the bottom of his shirt. He leaned over to push open the side door of the van. Since it was after midnight the streets were almost empty. He quietly walked up the steps to his apartment and disappeared into the building. In less than five minutes he returned to the van and jumped back in.

Then the van was off to Mr. Alvarado's place in order to pick up the rewards for their fearless effort of killing another human being. The van pulled to the curb in front of Alvarado's apartment where Wilson got out. Now he had a bounce in his step as he climbed the steps to Alvarado's apartment. He knocked on the door and waited. No one immediately came to the door and Wilson had a sinking feeling that he may have been duped. The longer he stood there his mind started contemplating negative thoughts. Then there was the faint sound of footsteps coming toward the door.

The door latch made a metallic sound as the front door swung open. Alvarado motioned him to come in. At the same time, he placed his index finger in front of his mouth and quietly said, "Shush." Wilson Sanchez was tempted to shout at the top of his voice, "We did it." Wilson realized that now wasn't the time to celebrate. Alvarado continued to give him a blank stare as he said, "Let me check with the wife."

Wilson handed back to Alvarado his cellphone that Wilson had borrowed from him. Immediately Alvarado flipped it open and dialed in the wife's number. There was no answer as Wilson stood next to him. As they patiently waited, Wilson wondered if he might have shot the wrong person.

Wilson was becoming agitated by the delay. Then Alvarado made contact with the wife. He asked if everything was okay. He directly asked the wife, "Then should I pay them?" He waited until she gave the green light. Alvarado said, "Gracias" and hung up. He walked into another room and came back with a stack of cash in 100- and 20-dollar bills.

Alvarado unceremoniously handed over the money. Wilson didn't know how to react. Should he stand there in front of Alvarado and count the money? Or should he act more like a macho executioner who had confidence that no one would dare short a genuine hitman like himself?

Wilson looked at the stack of bills and all he could think about was that $8,000 in cash was a huge amount of money. He grabbed the money and tried to stuff it in his pockets. When his pockets were crammed full, he used his hands to carry out the remaining amount. As he was about to walk out of Alvarado's apartment he stopped and turned in the direction of the old man who stood stooped over. Wilson didn't know what to say. Should he thank the old guy for the money? Or should he say, "If you need someone else knocked off let me know. It was a pleasure doing business with you."

Wilson couldn't think of the proper words for this occasion so he merely said, "I'll see you" and closed the door behind him. He made a beeline to his cohorts waiting in the van. After taking his seat in the van he told Monroy to start driving. They drove around the block and Wilson instructed Monroy to pull to the curb in a darkened area. Wilson turned to face the others and began pulling cash out of his pockets and placing it on the seat.

Wilson wanted to make sure that Alvarado hadn't cheated him on the total amount of $8,000. Although Wilson never paid attention in his math classes in school, he was now ready to test his math skills. The cash was mainly in hundred-dollar bills with several stacks of twenty-dollar bills. He started counting and placing the bills in various stacks. The other two guys were intently watching. Since this was more money than any of them had ever seen in their lives, they looked on in starry-eyed amazement. When Wilson had finished counting, he had a frown on his face. He counted again and seemed puzzled since the amount didn't add up to $8,000. But every time he continued, he came up $20.00 short. He asked his buddies to verify that he had been cheated out of $20.

Wilson was livid. How could the so-called middleman have cheated him the hitman out of the full amount? After everyone in the van had agreed that they had only $7,980, Wilson angrily announced to his colleagues that he was going to go back and confront Alvarado. However, his partners in crime took a more philosophic approach and tried to reason with him that $20 wasn't worth fighting over especially at this late hour. They mentioned that it would be better to discuss this shortage after smoking several joints of weed.

Monroy and Pablo tried to switch the subject to what they were most concerned about which was how much was Wilson going to pay them. Originally when Wilson had asked them to help him out, he mentioned that if he got $8,000, they would each get $1,000. Since Wilson was so mad at Alvarado for shorting him, he wasn't inclined to be so generous with his helpers. None of them had done any of the heavy lifting that Wilson had done.

This was the moment when Wilson showed his true colors. He counted out $500 and hand it to the Erik Monroy the driver. Then he paid his other colleague $500. It was apparent from their expressions that they were disappointed. As a result, he peeled off two more $20 bills and handed them the extra money as though he was giving them a tip. The other guys didn't know how to take it. Was Wilson trying to appear to be one of the last great spenders? Or was he trying to pay them off?

Wilson announced that it was 'Party Time' and gave Erik some of the money to go buy some weed. Then Wilson announced to his buddies that he wanted to go to Willis Barnes' (pseudonym) place to have him keep the money safe. This was a strange situation especially since Wilson was in a bad mood from being cheated out of some of his 'hit money.' Why would he want to hand over all that cash to another person? One might infer that even hitmen act illogical at times. Here Wilson was 100% trusting of one of his buddies who had nothing to do with the shooting.

When they made contact with Willis Barnes, Wilson gave him the blood money to hold for him. Willis willingly took all the cash into his house and placed it in a safe place. When he returned, the guys were ready to 'party.' They drove over to Manchester Park and parked in a secluded area. Within minutes the occupants of the van were higher than a kite in a March wind storm.

Within minutes everyone had mellowed out and the distribution of funds was no longer an issue on any of their minds. They had graduated from being punk kids from a tagging crew to professional hitmen. This was truly worth celebrating such a macho accomplishment in their young lives. The rest of the early morning was an unofficial contest to see who could get the highest. It wasn't until 8:00 in the morning that the group felt capable enough to leave the old beat-up van and venture home where they could crash in their own pads. Little did these three hitmen realized how their lives had forever been changed and they certainly hadn't been changed for the better.

CHAPTER 3 THEY WERE NOW IN ANOTHER LEAGUE

Now Wilson Sanchez, Erik Monroy and Pablo Alvarenga would no longer be considered the 'Three Amigos.' They had earned their stripes as tried-and-true hitmen. They had proved that they had the skill, experience and the courage to be hired killers. Their fellow 'tagging team' members would definitely show them more respect as individuals, especially for what they had achieved. What was uncanny was that each one of them thought of himself as a hitman in training. However, the only hitmen they knew about were those they had seen on the big silver screen or the boob tube.

The movie titled ***Hitman*** showed a character that our guys might have liked to emulate. However, they might prefer being compared to the two hitmen in the 1994 movie ***Pulp Fiction***. That movie had two memorable characters, one being Vincent Vega being played by John Travolta. This character was a slick hitman who spent most of his time reminiscing about his trip to Amsterdam. There he shot adrenaline into his boss's wife's heart, while taking out any targets that he was ordered to whack.

The other hitman in that movie was Jules Winnfield, played by Samuel Jackson. That person was totally different from his partner in crime. Both were good at their job and truly consummate professionals. This second guy was so cool and slick, yet if you pissed him off, he wouldn't hesitate pumping you full of lead. He didn't come across as a gun-toting monster but as a dude who could be hilarious since he liked to talk about his favorite topics: food and sex.

But as to the driver of the van, Erik Monroy, he fancied himself more as a Tom Cruise character from the 2004 movie ***Collateral*** who was an outright cold-blooded hitman. This hitman was decked out in white hair, without a humorous bone in his body. The Tom Cruise character tortured a helpless cab driver forcing him to drive him to all the targets that he was required to eliminate. Even though Cruise's character seemed ruthless and acted with reckless abandon, he had a softer gentler side when he came in contact with the other character's sick mother. The movie tried to convey that the most well-trained murderer could be beaten at his own game.

The last member of our hitman team was Pablo Alvarenga who was better known as 'Basic.' He could be described as similar to the hitman character in the movie ***'No Country for Old Men.'*** That movies' hitman was considered a coin-flipping hitman played by Javier Bardem. The Josh Brolin character was a welder who found the money and absconded with millions of dollars from a botched drug deal. This hitman differed from the hitmen portrayed in ***Pulp Fiction*** since he was an utterly emotionless killer who seemed unstoppable. What made him especially scary was that he came across as the closest thing to a human Terminator. Nothing could stop him from killing anyone who crossed his path.

It is one of those puzzling paradoxes as to why do people admire hitmen especially those depicted in movies. It may be that hitmen appear to live exciting lives. Or it may be the fact that hitmen give the aura of being all-powerful—the type of person that no one would want to mess with. These three guys from 81st Street now found themselves in a new world where they definitely could be labeled as someone who was SPECIAL.

Back in 2005, life was slightly different. The most popular movies of that year were ***The 40-Year-Old Virgin***, ***Harry Potter and the Goblet of Fire*** as well as ***Batman Begins***. It is safe to say that these novice hitmen hadn't seen any of them. There were several television programs that would have been helpful if the three hitmen had watched any one of them like ***CSI- Las Vegas, CSI-Miami, CSI – NY*** and ***NCIS***. Other similar cop programs were ***Without a Trace, Cold Cases, Law & Order: Special Victims Unit*** and ***Criminal Minds***. If these guys had paid attention to any of those programs, they would have realized that criminals eventually get caught.

The question was whether any of the hitmen were in tune with any of the top musical hits of 2005. There was the possibility that the hitmen would have heard some of 50 Cent's hits like ***Candy Shop*** and ***Disco Inferno***. But it was less likely they were influenced by Kelly Clarkson's ***Since U Been Gone*** or Gwen Stefani's hit ***Rich Girl***. Even though the hitmen may not have been involved in the popular culture they were aware of what was going on in the barrio.

It is doubtful that any of the hitmen were thoroughly aware of the biggest event taking place anywhere in the world on the date of April 9, 2005. As cosmopolitan as these three lads might have thought they were, none of them had received an invitation to the wedding of Charles, Prince of Wales, and Camilla, Duchess of Cornwall. The tying of the royal nuptials occurred in a civil ceremony at Windsor's Guildhall followed by a blessing at St George's Chapel in Windsor Castle. If these guys had been invited and attended, they wouldn't have been involved in the killing of Reynaldo Quijano on April 9th. Fate seems fickle at times.

CHAPTER 4 POLICE RESPOND

Within a minute of the shooting, a LAPD dispatcher received a phone call on their 911 emergency system. The caller claimed that some type of incident had occurred at Alcove and Stagg streets in the Sun Valley district. The caller indicated that there was a shooting and a person was motionless in a car. Immediately police units were dispatched to the intersection.

The first officer, Officer Higgins (pseudonym), to arrive noticed that a brown Mercedes was blocking Stagg Street. The officer exited his vehicle and proceeded closer to the car. The officer took his flashlight and shined it on the face of the driver who seemed to be slumped over with his head leaning to the left side of the headrest. He could barely make out a male face that wasn't moving with his eyes closed.

The officer could hear the engine running and the headlights were on. Since the area was dark the officer couldn't easily determine why the car was parked in this odd position. In order to determine what had happened, the officer approached closer the driver's door. As he did so, he could see the driver's side window had been shattered. From the appearance of the broken-out window, the officer assumed that the driver of the vehicle had been shot by someone outside of the vehicle.

Whether the driver was a suspect or victim was unknown to the officer. At that point the officer was trying to assess the situation. The police broadcast had been about 'shots fired.' Most of those calls are nothing more than an empty scene with all the parties long gone by the time the police arrive. This time Officer Higgins was coming upon a real crime scene which would require considerable investigation. He needed to let the station know what he had discovered.

But his first task was to check on the well-being of the driver. The officer shouted at the driver to turn off the engine. He didn't expect a response from the driver but did it anyway. After two shouts, the officer could see that the driver wasn't responding to his commands. When he was within an arm's length of the driver, the officer noticed blood stains on the driver's shirt.

As he stood by himself next to a car that was running, he recognized he had a dangerous situation to deal with. What should he do about the running car?

Should he attempt to turn the engine off? He knew he shouldn't do anything to disturb the crime scene. This even included the turning off the engine or even the headlights.

At that moment the officer knew he needed to further learn whether the driver required medical assistance. The officer moved forward to render aid to the driver. As the officer cautiously leaned in through the driver's window, he could see that the car was still in 'Drive' and it was only the victim's foot on the brake that was preventing the car from going forward.

This was the type of split-second decisions that police officers are called upon to make daily. If the officer tried to open the driver's door, the victim's body was likely to fall out taking the victim's foot off the brake and the car would be propelled forward possibly striking someone. Or even worse, the victim's foot could slide off of the brake and come to rest on the accelerator. The car would be catapulted forward plowing full speed into the house directly across the street.

The officer had come upon a delicate balancing act. From the officer's position he couldn't reach over the driver to disengage the car from the 'Drive' position. Officer Higgins didn't have a nano-second to reflect on the consequences of his actions. He thrust his right hand through the shatter driver's window hoping not to be seriously cut by the jagged shards of glass. His objective was to turn off the ignition. In order to be able to reach the keys in the ignition, he had to extend his arm as far as it could reach. In the process he had to lean his head outside the car. That meant that he had to face away from the steering column of the Mercedes.

The officer used his fingertips of his right hand to feel for the ignition key. After sliding his fingertips up and down the steering column he felt the key on the keychain and knew he was getting close to the ignition. As his fingers gripped the ignition key he froze. Which way should he turn the key to remove it from the ignition? He twisted it counter-clockwise and squeezed the key to remove it. Much to the relief of the officer, the engine went silent. The officer was never so happy to hear the sound of nothing.

Once the car was rendered safe, the officer checked on the driver's condition. As he pressed his two fingers on the victim's neck, he could feel no pulse. The officer continued to apply pressure on the neck. His fingers frantically moved all across the neck in hopes he could detect some type of heart beat even if it were faint.

At no point could he feel anything that resembled a pulse but he didn't want to make a mistake if there was any chance of life. As long as he had been a police officer he didn't cherish these moments when he had to make life-and-death decisions.

He needed to make a split-second decision. If he yanks the victim out of the vehicle in order to try to save his life, he had better make sure that the victim was savable. Because if the victim was truly dead the homicide detectives wouldn't want the patrol officer disturbing a crime scene by moving the victim. Or on the other hand, if the officer doesn't try to render aid when the victim was in dire need of medical assistance, he could be civilly sued for being negligent.

The officer was dangling in never-never land in which he could be wrong no matter what he did. He bent backwards to take a better look at the victim. Blood was gushing out of his body. His body wasn't moving or even twitching. The officer shook his own head slightly as he noticed more officers arriving. Now he wished he hadn't been the first to arrive at the crime scene.

The officer stepped back from the car and yelled for someone to call for the paramedics. Now that he had the victim's situation under control, he automatically did what he had been trained to do which was to secure the crime scene. He went over to his police unit and reached into the trunk and retrieved a roll of yellow emergency tape. Then he asked one of his fellow officers to help him cordon off the crime scene area with the tape. The first order of business was to preserve the crime scene. Obviously, the victim and the Mercedes should be included in the cordoned-off area. But the big question was what else should be included. When the officer shined his flashlight on the surface of the street, he noticed expended shell casings. He knew he should include all the area where he could see anything that looked like it could be evidence in a homicide case.

Officer Higgins didn't want to be accused by the homicide detectives of not sufficiently protecting the crime scene. That was why he told his colleagues to extend the yellow tape all the way to the intersection of Alcove and Stagg streets. That should be an adequate area to preserve. As the officer continued to stretch the crime scene tape on Alcove Street, he noticed some litter on the street. Should he include that in the so-called crime scene area? Since the trash was some distance away from the victim and Mercedes, the officer chose not to include it within the boundaries of the official crime scene.

In an abundance of caution, the officer decided to check out this piece of debris outside the cordoned off area. He wanted to cover his 'ass' so he walked over to where it was located. In doing so he stepped into a puddle of something in the street. Instantly the officer shined his flashlight on the liquid which had made a giant spot on the asphalt. Why this looked strange, was the fact that this liquid was next to a 'no parking' area. The curb was painted bright red since it was next to an intersection. Officer Higgins didn't know what to make of the puddle of fluid but he carefully sidestepped the mess and proceeded to the nondescript piece of trash.

In the dark he could barely make out what the object was. In order to figure out what the item was he used his flashlight to illuminate it. Often juveniles will buy fast food and when finished they irresponsibly toss the wrappers out of their car. Undoubtedly this litter was most likely some type of fast-food debris. However, it didn't look like fast-food wrappers and it didn't reflect like a cigarette pack. Also, the item wasn't wadded up like typical trash.

All he could see was a folded piece of paper. As the officer stood directly over the item, he couldn't figure out what it was. All that could be seen was a piece of paper with writing printed on it.

This piqued the officer's curiosity, so he leaned down and picked it up and unfolded it. His eyes glanced at it, but he couldn't comprehend what it was. It looked familiar but what was it?

His eyes noticed the wording 'Make Payment To' **The Gas Company** P.O. Box C Mont Pk Ca 91756. Like a light bulb going off in his brain, he recognized what it was - a gas utility bill.

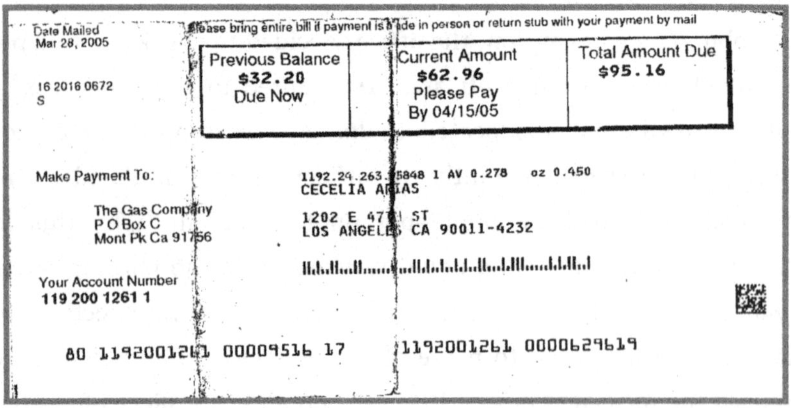
Date Mailed
Mar 28, 2005

Please bring entire bill if payment is made in person or return stub with your payment by mail

Previous Balance	Current Amount	Total Amount Due
$32.20 Due Now	$62.96 Please Pay By 04/15/05	$95.16

16 2016 0672
S

Make Payment To:

The Gas Company
P O Box C
Mont Pk Ca 91756

1192.24.263.15848 1 AV 0.278 oz 0.450
CECELIA ARIAS
1202 E 47TH ST
LOS ANGELES CA 90011-4232

Your Account Number
119 200 1261 1

80 1192001261 00009516 17 1192001261 0000629619

His first reaction was that it was trash that had been blown out of someone's trash can. But like most cops he was intrigued as to why this gas bill was in the street. That was when he looked at the address on the utility bill which was 202 E 47th St, Los Angeles, CA. That address location didn't make sense.

Years earlier the officer had worked the South-Central LA area and was familiar with the area around the location listed on the gas bill. This address was for a house over ten miles away. How could this gas bill end up in the middle of the street in the San Fernando Valley? This patrol officer stopped in his tracks and smiled to himself. He came back to reality and recognized he was overanalyzing the situation. He took the gas bill and replaced it back where he had found it.

The officer was tired but he couldn't think of a scenario how and why was this gas bill on a street in the San Fernando Valley. When the supervising patrol sergeant arrived on scene, the officer made an offhanded comment that he had found a gas utility bill in the street. Officer Higgins didn't want to make a big deal out of the gas bill but what the hell could it be all about. He bucked it up the totem pole. The guys with the stripes and detectives could do whatever they wanted to do with this gas bill which was nothing more than a piece of trash.

Within the hour someone from the detective bureau had responded to the crime scene. The patrol officers were greatly relieved when they saw the arrival of one of the detectives. There is a 'love-hate' relationship between the patrol officers and the detectives. Often the detectives come late on the scene and they can be highly critical of what the initial officers should have and shouldn't have done. The harried patrol officer is often faced with a confusing situation when responding to radio call. Frequently it takes time to figure out what is actually going on. It is easy for a detective who comes on the scene after things have settled down, to second-guess the original patrol officer for what he or she may have done or not done.

CHAPTER 5 THE DICKS ARRIVE

There's an old adage that the first 48 hours after a homicide are the most critical time to find evidence and witnesses. It is also the best time to get statements from all the parties involved. This present situation was no exception. Fortunately, the head of the homicide detectives for North Hollywood Division, Detective Carson (pseudonym), instantly responded to the crime scene. He was a well-seasoned homicide detective who knew exactly what had to be done ASAP. With his early involvement in the case he had the power and authority to quickly assign other detectives to do follow-up investigation.

A side benefit of having Detective Carson at the crime scene was that he recognized the importance of the patrol officers and had developed a respectable working rapport with those officers assigned to North Hollywood Division. Upon his arrival, he contacted the supervising sergeant on the scene and asked the usual question: "What do we have here?" The sergeant pointed to the Mercedes and said that the deceased was still in the driver's seat. The sergeant related that when the first patrol officers arrived, the vehicle's engine was running and the car was still in the 'Drive' position.

The detective's next question was, "Who's the dude in the car?" The sergeant smiled and said, "That's for you to find out." He went on to recount that his patrol officers didn't want to disturb the body so they hadn't gone through his pockets looking for the victim's wallet. "So, who is the vehicle registered to?" The sergeant re-counted that he was having one of his officers run the license plate through DMV to find out who was the RO (registered owner).

The sergeant quickly responded that there were several expended shell casings on the street near the vehicle. That prompted the detective to ask if any gun had been recovered, to which the sergeant shook his head and said, "Nope." The next few questions related to the possibility of any witnesses to the shooting. Again, the sergeant grinned and said that no one had come forward to indicate they had seen anything. Since it had occurred during the early morning hours, he warned that eye-witnesses were going to be in short supply.

The head detective stood in the middle of the street staring at the sergeant. The detective said in the most sarcastic voice he could muster up at this hour, "You mean to tell me you don't know who was killed or the reason for the killing, and on top of that you have no physical evidence except for four lousy shell casings?" The sergeant with a slight chuckle responded by saying, "Wait a minute, I forgot to tell you we found a piece of trash in the street." The detective didn't know how to reply, so he said, "What's the big deal about this piece of rubbish?"

The sergeant responded by saying, "One of my officers found something on the street that looked like a utility bill. It is doubtful that it has any relevance to this case but I thought I would throw it in since there isn't much to go on." The Sergeant with a smug look on his face glanced over to Detective Carson and replied, "This is why you are paid the big bucks since you seem to be able to make a silk purse out of a sow's ear."

Detective Carson frowned at the sergeant's mockery and turned away and picked up his radio and called the station. He ordered whoever was next up on the night duty detectives' roaster to be directed to head to the crime scene.

In short order, Detective Joe Espinosa (pseudonym) arrived and contacted his boss Detective Carson who updated him on the facts that he knew. At Carson's direction he took charge of marking and collecting the evidence. Detective Espinosa proceeded to the Mercedes to survey where the shooting occurred. As he approached, he could clearly see the expended shell casings on the asphalt street surface. With his flashlight he could spot all four shell casings.

Since the investigation could take hours, he decided to mark on the pavement exactly where each shell casing was located. His concern was someone might kick one of the casing out of its original position. He knew that the forensic technicians and the photographer would place evidence identification numbers next to every piece of evidence.

Although marking and photographing all the evidence is a tedious task, it can be crucial later on in proving up certain facts at trial. Detective Espinosa noticed that the shell casings were in a linear or straight-line row. Since there were four shell casings, the detective knew that the murder weapon was an automatic not a revolver handgun. Also, he knew from his police training that most automatics expel the used shell casing to the right of the shooter.

As he picked up the shell casings and examined them, he determined that they were 9mm ammunition. What was unusual about the casings was the fact that they were from different manufacturers. One was a Winchester 9mm Lugar and another was a Fiocchi Brand 9mm. What did the use of different brands of ammunition tell the detective? Really not much, except it is not unusual in gang shootings to have mixed ammo. The reason for this is that gang shooters often grab whatever ammo they can find. They aren't like professional target shooters who prefer certain brands for their unique characteristics and accuracy.

While looking for more shell casings, the detective opened the driver's side door. The inside of the car was covered with shards of glass. To the detective's surprise he saw a projectile from one of the casings lying on the seat next to the victim. He surmised that the shooter was within a few feet when he fired the last shot.

After analyzing all the locations of the casings, the detective came to the opinion that the shooter approached the car when it was parallel to the curb and shot at the victim four times after which the car turned to the left and ended up perpendicular to the street.

No handgun or any weapon was found on the victim or anywhere inside the Mercedes. The only thing in the victim's jacket pocket was a cellphone. When his pants were checked they found a wallet and some money with several coins and keys.

Detective Timothy Kirby (pseudonym) was one of the unlucky detectives whose number came up that night. In little more than an hour he was weaving his way through the lonely streets of this blue-collar residential area of Sun Valley. This community is definitely a nondescript area that has seen highs and some deep lows. During the WWII period, this residential area was the home for many engineers and assemblers for the aviation industry. The Lockheed company had a massive aircraft plant in the area specializing in the building of the infamous P-38 Lightning.

This aircraft had a very distinctive shape with twin booms and a central nacelle containing the cockpit and armament. The P-38 was responsible for shooting down more Japanese aircraft than any other US aircraft.

The Lockheed plant was so valuable to the Allies that he was covered by camouflage so enemy aircraft couldn't bomb it. The War Department did an incredible job of covering the acres of manufacturing buildings with burlap tarpaulin painted to depict a rural area with fake trees and shrubs.

The plant was adjacent to an airport which was only two blocks from the crime scene. This airport had gone by so many names no one really knows its proper name. Over the years, it was called the United Airport, Union Air Terminal, Lockheed Air Terminal, Hollywood-Burbank Airport, Burbank-Glendale-Pasadena Airport, Bob Hope Airport and in 2016 it reverted back to being officially called the Hollywood Burbank Airport.

The detective recalled all the controversy surrounding this little postage-stamp airport. He remembered that none of the neighbors wanted it because of the noise and the smell of the jet exhaust. The main portion of the airport is located in the city of Burbank. When the airport needed to expand one of the runways, they had to build a third of the runway on property that was located in the City of Los Angeles. This causes all sorts of jurisdiction issues, when something happens on that runway.

Detective Kirby was trying to picture the area of Arcola and Stagg streets and how close it was to the airport. He couldn't recollect any serious criminal problems that the North Hollywood LAPD Division had ever responded in this area of Sun Valley. His partner Detective Thompson (pseudonym) also got called out and met Detective Kirby at the crime scene. After arriving they both went over to their boss Detective Carson and received a briefing on the facts and what had already been done. Since Detective Espinosa was deeply involved with the crime scene, these new detectives decided to concentrate their effort on finding and interviewing any eyewitnesses.

At 2:15 in the morning who do you start interviewing? Initially you begin with anyone standing around. When that didn't prove fruitful the detectives contacted the dispatcher to learn who had called in the incident.

The first caller was a neighbor, Ethan Selzer, who lived two houses south of the shooting location. He was contacted and stated that he had been working on his computer. He explained that he had found that the early morning hours are the best time to work on his computer. At that time of night there weren't distractions from others and no phone calls to interrupt his train of thought. Especially in this part of town, it can be dead silent after midnight.

That was why he was shocked to hear the gunfire shortly after midnight. It sounded like two to four shots which was followed by a 20-second delay when he heard the roar of vehicle drive down Stagg Street. Mr. Selzer wanted to be helpful but he didn't look outside at the time of the shooting. He couldn't identify the shooter or even the type of vehicle used. The detectives tried to canvass the neighborhood but were confronted with tired residents who didn't appreciate being awakened in the early morning hours.

Around 2:30 p.m. all the detectives regrouped and went over what they had uncovered. They hadn't found any eyewitnesses but the coroner investigator had removed the victim's wallet and determined that his name was Reynaldo Quijano. Further they learned he lived in the house directly behind the Mercedes. What was peculiar was that no one from that house had come out and asked what was going on. Detective Kirby indicated that he would contact whoever was living in the house as soon as he had finished up with the neighbors.

When the detectives had talked to the dispatcher, she said that a woman by the name of Sally Talles (pseudonym) had made a 9-1-1 call regarding this incident. The two detectives headed over to that caller's residence to see if she was available to talk.

CHAPTER 6 THE GODSEND WITNESS SALLY TALLES

Detective Kirby headed down Stagg Street to Ms. Talles' house. As he approached, he noticed in the driveway a pickup truck and car. As he squeezed between the vehicles, he was pleased to see the interior lights were on in the house. That meant that he wasn't going to have to wake someone up. Instead of ringing the doorbell he gently knocked on the wooden door. After not receiving any answer he rapped on the door harder and this time he got the attention of the family dog who announced his presence.

Moments later someone inside said, "Who is it?" In the most pleasant voice, he could marshal up at this early hour Detective Kirby replied, "It's the police." Within seconds a young petite woman opened the door just a crack and peered out. The detective displayed his badge in one hand while holding a flashlight in the other. Hesitating for a moment the women said, "Come on in, I was kind of expecting you." She motioned them toward the living room and flipped on a light switch which illuminated the room.

Detective Kirby said that he would like to hear from her as to what she knew about the shooting. Sally hesitated for a moment not knowing what she should say. With a pained look on her face, she indicated that she didn't want to get involved. She exclaimed that she wasn't the 'hero type' and was scared to death that the guys in the van might come after her.

Hearing those few words the Detective Kirby recognized that he had 'hit pay dirt.' It was obvious from her statement that she had seen some part of the shooting. This detective had been in this type of situation many times and he understood he needed to calm the witness down and give her some assurance that anything she said wouldn't jeopardize her safety. He explained that whatever she said would be kept confidential. All he wanted from her was some help trying to figure out what happened.

"Could you just tell me what you saw or heard earlier this morning?" With that she pointed to a chair and said, "Okay have a seat and I will tell you what I know." The detective sat down in one of the overstuffed chairs and took out his notebook with his pen ready.

As she sat on the edge of the chair, she started reciting the facts. "I got off work and drove home. It was about 12:15 a.m. when I pulled into my driveway and parked my car. I was on my cellphone talking to a friend. After finishing talking to her, I opened my car door to get out. All of sudden I heard several gunshots and looked in the direction of the gunfire."

She paused for a moment to gather her thoughts and expressed to the detective that she was worried stiff. She related that she saw a person running toward a van that seemed to be in the middle of the intersection. Because it was dark out, she couldn't see the face of the runner. The best she could recall was that he had on some type of dusky color hoodie. She couldn't say with certainty that it was a male but the way it ran and size of its body she inferred it was a guy.

When this person reached the van, he seemed to jump in on the passenger side. Although she couldn't actually see him get in since she had to view this through the driver's side of the van. All of a sudden, the van made an abrupt left turn heading down her street on which she lived. Immediately, Sally panicked, thinking that if the suspects saw her as a witness, they would try to kill her. She further described that out of desperation she bent down to hide herself behind her father's pickup truck which was parked in the driveway. She listened intently in hopes that the suspects would drive on by and leave her alone.

It seemed like an eternity as the van raced by her driveway. She didn't want to be noticed by the shooters so she froze in place. Within seconds the van was gone. By then, Sally got enough courage to rise up from her hiding position and sprint as fast as she could toward her front door. With her house key she nervously tried to stick it in the lock but somehow, she couldn't get it in the keyhole. As her hands were shaking, she tried to concentrate on the simple task of opening the door. Eventually she was successful and ran into her house.

She had her phone in one hand as she moved from room to room ending up in her bedroom. She maneuvered toward the window in the bedroom so she could gain a view of the street. There she could see the car parked in the middle of the street. She dialed 9-1-1. When the dispatcher asked her, what was the purpose of her emergency, she didn't know how to respond. Her reaction was that she didn't have any emergency but only wanted to inform the police that something unusual had happened in her neighborhood.

She told the dispatcher she could see a car in the middle of the street with its lights on. She related that she had heard three or four gunshots and saw a person get into some type of van which took off down her street. The dispatcher informed her that she would dispatch police units to check out the situation. Before hanging up the dispatcher obtained Sally's phone number and her specific address.

After Detective Kirby had listened to Sally's story, he asked her what else did you see that you thought was unusual? She thought for a moment and said that she didn't know if it was important but there was something earlier that had caught her attention. The detective asked, "What was that?" Sally leaned back in the chair and her eyes stared up to the ceiling. After clearing her throat, she explained that when she was driving home down Stagg Street as she approached intersection, she noticed on Arcola a van illegally parked in a red 'no parking' zone.

She went on to say that in all the years she had lived there she had never seen a vehicle parked there. She explained that the street is narrow in that area and the city had the curb painted red to prevent anyone from parking at that spot. One of the reasons why she noticed the van was that it was directly under a street light. The detective interrupted Sally by asking if she got a good look at this van. She nodded in the affirmative. Then she tried to recollect the appearance of the vehicle. Nothing seemed to stand out in her mind as to how to describe it. She continually repeated that she was certain it was a van. All she could recollect was that it was a nondescript dirty brown color.

The detective asked the crucial question which was whether she saw the license plate number of the van. He was hoping that this one witness was going to provide the key to solving this case. Sally smiled and chuckled to herself and said, "I saw the rear of the van and undoubtedly saw the license number but I have no recollection of it." Detective Kirby couldn't help but come to grips with the fact that this homicide wasn't going to be solved the easy way.

He didn't want the witness to feel guilty for not being observant enough to notice and write down the license number. He asked, "Okay, what do you remember about the van?" Sally took a moment to gather her thoughts. Again, she looked up toward the ceiling as though she was going to gain some type of inspiration from above. Then slowly she began her answer. Somehow in her mind she remembered the van to be old and dirty. The detective asked her to try to give him a description of the van from the front to the back and sides.

Sally was tired since it was late into the early morning hours. She told the detective that the entire situation had made her hyper and she couldn't sleep even though she was tired. She stopped talking and looked as though she was in deep thought. All of a sudden, she tried to find words to describe the fact that there was something covering one of the side windows of the van. She said, "There was a white or light-colored covering over the side window of the van."

Detective Kirby was also tired but was trying to listen intently to the witness. He wrote down in his notes that the van was described as old and it had a window covered with a light-colored paper or plastic. He wanted to be sure where she had seen the van. He asked her to step outside and point to the area where she saw the parked van. As she stood in her driveway, she pointed to the location on Arcola Avenue where the van had been parked in the red zone.

Before leaving Sally's house the detective asked one more time if she thought she could identify the shooter or anyone in the van. The witness shrugged her shoulders and slowly shook her head. She sincerely said to the detective, "I'm sorry but I really didn't get a good look at any of their faces." Detective Kirby gave Sally a half smile and said, "I'm sorry to have bothered you, thanks for the information," With that said Sally walked back into her house as the detective continued to walk down the empty sidewalk back to the crime scene.

CHAPTER 7- ASSESSMENT OF WHAT EVIDENCE THEY HAD

When Detective Kirby returned to the crime scene, he lifted up the yellow tape in order not to tear it. He went over to his boss, the head of the detectives, and asked the question, "Well, what have we come up with?" He was told that the Forensic photographer had finished up and the shell casings had been picked up and placed in evidence envelopes. The coroner had come and removed the victim's body. As a result, it was discovered that the victim lived in the house behind the Mercedes at 727 Arcola Avenue.

He was told that the occupants of the house were notified that the victim was deceased. This seemed surprising that the occupants hadn't come out to inform the police that the victim lived there. Detective Kirby was told that he should see if he could interview the occupants. He turned around and proceeded to the victim's home. While standing at the front door he knocked and waited for a response. He could see that the lights were on inside but no one was coming to the door.

The detective knocked harder on the door and said, "Police, please open up." Eventually, a middle-aged woman came to the door and opened it slightly. She said, "What do you want?" He replied, "We would like to talk to you about the man who had been shot." Then the woman fully opened the door and told him to come in. She directed the detective to the living room where they both sat down. Initially, he asked her name. Then she said that she was Maria Quijano.

The detective again removed a notepad from his pocket and wrote down her name. He inquired as to her relationship to the deceased. She said that he was her husband. What caught the detective by surprise was the fact that this victim's wife exhibited no emotion even though she had just been notified of her husband's death. Detective Kirby had been in similar situations when a person was informed of the demise of their spouse and most people became distraught and often became hysterical.

However, this wife looked more frightened then hysterical. The detective didn't know what to think. His first group of questions dealt with her not reacting to the hearing of gunfire just outside her door. She looked in disbelief when told about the gunshots. She claimed she didn't hear any such thing. Then she was further asked whether she had heard the sirens from the numerous police units and an ambulance which had responded to the location.

She shook her head indicating that she hadn't heard anything. Her explanation was that she was in the back bedroom of the house. She further stated that she had her TV on and **she had fallen asleep around 8:00 p.m.** The detective didn't want to dwell on her lack of responsiveness and absence of any emotion. He shifted the questioning to when she had last seen her husband.

She started talking about going to the bank with him during the morning. It had something to do with her and him having separate bank accounts. She explained that on the next day he was leaving for a month long visit his home country El Salvador. After leaving the bank they returned home and he left for work. She didn't see him return to the house which he generally did each night. His routine was to go to the kitchen and grab a slice of bread and a glass of milk. From there he would retreat to their master bedroom where he spent most of his time watching television.

However, this evening she had not heard him come home and just assumed he had followed his usual routine. Since she couldn't give much insight as to her husband's whereabouts, the detective switched to the couple's personal relationship. He felt this might not be a good time to make such an inquiry.

The detective had a gut feeling that things weren't adding up. Considering the victim's age, this homicide didn't seem to be GANG related. Since the victim had his wallet on him with considerable cash and credit cards, this didn't have the ear markings of a ROBBERY. There was no evidence of a FIGHTING situation since the shooting didn't occur in a bar or where people have confrontations with each other. Even the possibility of ROAD RAGE didn't fit the factual situation, since it involved a person in a car in front of his house.

The detective was totally at a loss to determine a MOTIVE for the shooting of the victim. Now he wanted to pursue the possibility that the killing was motivated by FINANCIAL GAIN by the wife or someone else. The other possibility was that it was related to some type of DOMESTIC VIOLENCE. This didn't seem to be a real possibility since most DV cases involve a male spouse attacking or killing a female spouse.

With this mixed bag the detective started asking the wife further background questions. He asked about their marriage as to whether they were having problems. In most situations the detective would not have been so direct. Nonetheless the wife didn't seem to be the grieving widow type. Questions under the present situation didn't appear to be uncalled for.

In order to gain some insight into their relationship the detective started at the beginning. He asked when and where did the two of them meet? She indicated that she met her husband, Reynaldo, in El Salvador and shortly thereafter they were married in 1990. They didn't have any children between the two of them. However, she had a son and a daughter by two different men.

The detective could sense that the wife was conflicted when describing their marriage. At first, she said, "My husband and I had a good relationship. He treated me as a 'princess' around the house." Then she went on to admit that she believed that her husband was having an affair with a younger woman. She believed that this extramarital affair had resulted in the birth of a child.

To support her belief, she claimed that more recently she was receiving threatening phone calls from his girlfriend. At that point the detective asked if she had any thoughts of divorcing her husband. She admitted that she had such conversations with her son, Tony Herrera (pseudonym) about divorcing her husband. But with all the problems she still decided to stay married to Reynaldo.

After spending over an hour interviewing Maria, the wife, the detective thought that asking more questions wasn't going to reveal anything more about what had just happened. He picked up his notebook and stood up and thanked her for her time. He glanced down at his notebook and could see that he had numerous question marks with blank lines after them. Just as an afterthought the detective asked her for her phone number.

She indicated that she used her cellphone for all communication with others. She told him the number was (818) 919-2038 (pseudonym). So there would be no ambiguity the detective summarized the use of the wife's phone by saying, "You and no one else used your cellphone after you fell asleep around 8:00 p.m. tonight?" The wife listened to the question and shook her head in the negative. The detective reiterated that her phone had not been used. She uttered the word "NO" loud and clear.

The detective thought maybe it was because it was 3:00 a.m. and he was tired. Or maybe this victim's wife was demonstrating a different form of grieving he hadn't seen from other homicide victims' spouses. Since he was already inside the house, he casually asked Maria if her daughter, Dorthey Perez (pseudonym), was available to talk to him. With a slight hesitation, Maria got up from the chair and stated, "Let me see?" She walked toward the rear of the house and disappeared into a closed room.

After a several-minute delay a wide-eyed 17-year-old female came out of the back room slowly moving toward the detective. With a muted voice she asked the detective, "What do you need from me?" The detective hastily responded that all he needed was some basic information from everyone who was in the house at the time of the shooting. He assured her it would only take a minute or two.

She said, "Okay." At that point the detective nodded to one of the chairs and she walked over and sat down. The detective started asking her for her full name and how long she had lived in the house with her mother. Since her mother Maria hadn't returned to the room, the detective wanted to get the daughter's understanding of the facts.

He asked her when she got home that night. The daughter, Dorthey, replied that she got off work and came directly home. She tried to reconstruct what time it was. Her best estimate was sometime around 10:25 p.m. She explained that she remembered that Reynaldo's brown Mercedes was parked in front of the house. She didn't pay that much attention to whether Reynaldo was in the car. But her recollection was that the car appeared to be empty.

When asked about Reynaldo's whereabouts, she said she never saw him that night but believed that she heard him talking in the master bedroom he shared with her mother, Maria. She told the detective that she was tired and went to bed and fell asleep. The next thing she remembered was waking up to the sound of several gunshots. What caught her attention was that the family dog began barking and wouldn't stop. She estimated that it was 12:15 a.m. when she heard her mother, Maria, trying to shoo the dog from barking. Within a minute or so the dog calmed down and she went back to sleep.

This information didn't sit well with the detective. Why did the wife say that she didn't hear any gunshots while the daughter claimed she did hear gunfire? This wasn't adding up. What could be the reason for this discrepancy? Is the wife lying or merely confused? If the detective thought this case was going to be a challenging case, all of a sudden, he was getting the picture that not everything was what it seemed.

CHAPTER 8–TIME TO FOLLOW UP

After the conversation with the wife the detective had a disconcerting feeling about the wife but there was no evidence that indicated that she was the person who shot her husband. When Detective Kirby questioned the witness Sally, she believed that the person running to the van was a male even though she couldn't identify that person.

Detective Kirby met with the other detectives and they reviewed what they had come up with during those early morning hours of April 10, 2005. The forensic evidence proved nothing. There were no likely latent prints on the Mercedes since the evidence indicated that the shooter ran up to the car without having made contact with it. There was no likely DNA evidence again since the shooter didn't touch or drop anything at the crime scene.

There was no evidence that there was some type of heated argument between the victim and someone else. All the witnesses who had been spoken to claimed that they hadn't heard any yelling or scream by anyone at or before the shooting. The only forensic evidence was four expended shell casings and one projectile all of which were useless unless the handgun was found. Often in gang cases the ballistic evidence can be compared to other gang shootings to find a match even though the gun is never recovered. Since this case didn't appear to be gang-related, there were no other shootings to compare the casings and projectile to.

Unfortunately, this case wasn't lending itself to a swift conclusion, since there was no useable forensic evidence and no identification by witnesses.

The detectives were at a lost. All they had was a piece of trash found on the street over 100 feet away from the shooting. Detective Kirby asked to see the recovered piece of trash. One of the CSI techs handed him the item. He glanced at this Gas Bill which had a person's name and address. What does this all mean?

Three days later on April 13, 2005, Detective Kirby had become frustrated with the pace of the investigation. There hadn't been any break in this Quijano case. He was sitting at his cluttered detective desk filled with stacks of police reports and Blue Murder books from pending homicides. Then he remembered that the witness Sally had mentioned that she had seen a van parked in the red zone exactly were the gas bill was found. Could this gas bill be connected to the van that the shooter used to get away? Since the detectives didn't have any new workable leads, Detective Kirby thought why not check out the address listed on the gas bill.

He saw that Detective Haines (pseudonym) was sitting at his desk. He walked over to him and said, "Let's go down to South-Central to check out this crazy gas bill that was found at the Quijano crime scene." The two of them went out of the station and got in one of the 'dicks' Crown Vic's (a Ford Crown Victoria unmarked detective car). The two of them drove out of the North Hollywood station and headed toward the on-ramp for the Hollywood Freeway headed for the Civic Center.

Since it was mid-day, this part of the Hollywood Freeway flowed smoothly as it had been planned to function. However, during the rush hour it is a string of cars moving at a snail's pace. The detectives maneuvered their dick car into the fast lane as they approached the Ventura Freeway. After that, the Hollywood Freeway starts the transition from the San Fernando Valley to the mainland section of Los Angeles. At this point they were at the top of the Cahuenga Pass which connects the two parts of LA.

If it weren't for the annexation of the San Fernando Valley by the sleepy city of the Angels back in 1928, this vast metropolis would never have become the second largest city in the USA. The residents of the San Fernando Valley think of themselves as the step-children of the city of Los Angeles.

SEPARATION

The Valley residents see the major part of the LA city budget going to the occupants of South-Central LA. There is no question that the bulk of the police budget is spent in the South-Central area of Los Angeles and the Valley is definitely shortchanged. The resentment was so strong that in 2002 the residents of the San Fernando Valley tried to secede from the city of LA and create a separate city. This secession movement didn't succeed but it left many Valley residents resentful of their southern neighbors.

While starting down the Cahuenga Pass the detectives couldn't miss the gigantic sign announcing the entrance to Universal Studios. Back in 1915, motion pictures were being produced in what was then a rural area of Los Angeles. Over the years the studio has grown in size with its extensive Back Lot.

The studio recognized that the public would pay 25 cents to visit where motion pictures were made. By 1962, MCA took over the studio and recognized the profitability of studio tours. They noticed how successful the Walt Disney's theme park, Disneyland, had become. With small studio trams they could whisk tourists through the streets containing the old movie props like the old city hall from movies like ***Back to the Future*** and the notorious Bates Motel in the movie ***Pysco***. Today, Universal Studio tours are one of the main tourist attractions for L.A.

The detectives continued to cruise down the Cahuenga Pass and had to slow on the curve in the freeway where you can see the Hollywood Bowl to the right and to the left is the Pilgrimage Theatre with its giant imposing white cross on top of the hill overlooking Hollywood.

Back in 1921, some arty people of the city wanted to find a place where musicians and actors could give performances out in the open. They were looking for a natural hillside that was in a shaded canyon where they could create an amphitheater. They decided to use an area in the Cahuenga Pass called 'Daisy Dell' in Bolton Canyon.

The founder of the Hollywood Bowl project was Christine Stevenson who was the wealthy heiress of the Pittsburgh Paint Company. She and the Art Alliance group acquired the land and started rehearsing for the first play which dealt with a religious theme. Even before the first play debuted the majority of the group didn't want the venue to be strictly used for religious plays. This didn't sit well with the rich Pittsburg Paint heiress who was used to getting her way. She decided to leave the Hollywood Bowl project and merely walked across the Cahuenga Pass and purchased 29 acres on the east side where she built a new amphitheater named the Pilgrimage Theatre for her religious plays.

It seems peculiar that the same person, Mrs. Stevenson, was the founder of both amphitheaters. The Hollywood Bowl started modestly with a wooden stage and bench seating. Not until 1929 was a shell created over the stage with fixed seating. Today the Bowl seats 18,000 and is world famous for the artistic talent that performs there.

There is nothing more enchanting then sitting out under the stars listening to the most popular singers and musicians performing. There are the highbrow classic nights followed by the heavy metal nights in which the intoxicating scent of pot permeates the air as the audience seems to mellow out.

However, the Pilgrimage Theatre, now called the John Anson Ford Amphitheater, still sits on the east side of the Cahuenga Pass and can seat an audience of 1,400 and is used to provide a place for new musicians and actors to perform.

Mrs. Stevenson, the rich heiress, was recognized for her zeal to perform religious plays and was memorialized by erecting a 32-foot-high steel cross on the hill overlooking her second amphitheater.

Later her estate gave the Pilgrimage Theatre to the County of Los Angeles, which has maintained the amphitheater since 1940. Strangely enough Christine Stevenson continued to cause controversy decades after her death. Several groups have sued the County for maintaining the giant cross on government land. Fortunately, the Hollywood Pilgrimage Memorial Monument Association was created to take possession of the land where the cross is located and they legally maintain the cross. As a result, this colossal cross is forever looking down on all the lost souls in Hollywood.

As the detectives in their dick's car sped down the Hollywood Freeway, they had one last glance of the large cross. They could see in the background the **HOLLYWOOD** sign blazoned on the hillside. Back in 1923 the sign read HOLLYWOODLAND to promote a new residential development which advertised to be a superb environment without excessive cost. The developer erected on the south face of Mount Lee the letters 50 feet high and the sign was covered with 4,000 light bulbs with the words 'HOLLY', 'WOOD', and 'LAND' lighting up individually and then as a whole. The sign was intended to last a year and be torn down after the houses had been sold. However, it became a trademark for the city and the letters 'LAND' were scrapped and it became the symbol for the new entertainment capital.

The detectives quickly rolled through Hollywood community on the Hollywood Freeway which was built in 1924 when Angelinos decided on creating a ‘stop-free express highway’ between downtown Los Angeles and the San Fernando Valley. The first segment was a one-and-a-half-mile stretch comprising the Cahuenga Pass which the detectives had passed through. When this segment was opened, it had trolleys running down the center of the freeway. As the detective’s ‘Crown Vic’ passed under Hollywood Blvd, they passed over the section that had been constructed in 1954.

Back then the new freeway was controversial since it cut a path through houses and apartment buildings that had to be torn down displacing many residents. Now decades later the detectives could travel 70 miles an hour from the San Fernando Valley to Downtown LA on a smooth highway without any bumps in the road. However, this section of the Hollywood Freeway does have a few bumps that only homicide detectives can feel.

The reason is that the old-time detectives think about all the excavating that was done during the construction of the freeway in the 1955. That was when the LA homicide detectives were in search of the body of Mrs. Scott, a wealthy socialite who disappeared without a trace. Her husband L. Ewing Scott was accused of killing her and many believed that she was buried somewhere under the Hollywood Freeway during its construction phase. He was prosecuted for Murder entirely based on circumstantial evidence.

Since no one is going to dig up the Hollywood Freeway to look for Mrs. Scott's body, the bumps in the road will forever be a mystery as to what may be causing them. Shortly the detective's 'Crown Vic' entered the interchange leaving the Hollywood Freeway behind and rolling down the Harbor Freeway.

After World War II the smaller and older homes in the South-Central area were less desirable when the suburban housing boom began. That permitted the African American (Black) members to be able to afford homes in South-Central. When the 1962 LA Riots occurred, the Black Community had taken over South-Central. However, the devastation created by this civil unrest encouraged Blacks to look for safer places to live in the outlying areas. By the 1990s there was an immigration wave that crashed over the city of LA. Year by year the Hispanic immigrants pushed out the majority of Blacks out of the area until South-Central became one of the largest Hispanic communities in the USA.

During these transition years, the LAPD officers felt the brunt of the tension between the Black and Hispanic communities. This was mainly seen as rivalries between the Black gangs trying to protect their turf as the Hispanic gangs continued to encroach block by block until the Hispanics were in control.

Both officers could remember how this area had changed over the years. They pulled off the Harbor Freeway on to a small off-ramp. At the signal they had to turn left and went under the Harbor Freeway. In order to reach the address on the gas bill of 202 E. 47 Street, they had to proceed ten blocks to the East. The area was made up of older wooden structures that need some attention such as paint or repair as real estate brokers refer to as 'deferred maintenance.'

Most residents are blue collar workers and they live from paycheck to paycheck. Landscaping their front yard would be a low priority for most of them. What is a high priority is steel bars over their windows and doors. These South-Central residents can't afford the luxury of homeowners' insurance so they try to make their house a fortress to discourage burglars.

From the standpoint of the cops this is an area made up of hardworking people requiring both the father and mother to work outside the home. As a result, the children are often left unattended during the day. During the early teenage years, the youth come in contact with the members of the local gangs. Because these youth have time on their hands, they easily fall into the gang culture. Other youths feel compelled to join a gang in order to guarantee protection. The graffiti on the cinder block walls or garage doors informs the residents who controls this turf.

The cops well know how good kids succumb to the gang temptation. But there is no simple solution. Millions of dollars have been spent on Gang Intervention and Community Policing. This is like a bandage on a hemorrhage wound in that it can stop a little bleeding but doesn't come close to solving the problem.

The detectives had wishful thinking that the described van would be parked in the driveway or in front of the residence listed on the gas bill. As the 'dick's' 'Crown Vic' slowly rolled by the address they observed some dirty old vehicles but no brown van. That was disappointing so they circled the block and came back on the other side glancing at any and all vehicles in sight.

Then the two detectives pulled over and parked where they could see the front door of the residence in question. They were wondering whether they should go to the house and speak to the resident named on the gas bill. But the detectives hesitated since they didn't want to blow their cover. Their thinking was that if they made personal contact, the owner or user of the van could hide it so they would never be able to inspect it.

After spending nearly, a half an hour waiting to see if the van appeared, the detectives agreed that this wasn't a wise use of their time. They had phone calls to make and forensic reports to review. As homicide detectives knew all too well, they needed to be patient and wait for another opportunity to locate that mysterious old brown van.

CHAPTER 9 –BINGO– WE HAVE FOUND IT

Four days later on April 17, 2005, Detective Kirby was discouraged that no big break had occurred in the Quijano case. He was hoping for a 'Eureka' moment and again he thought about the gas bill address. Could that unlock this case for him? He hadn't been lucky winning the multi-million Lotto but somehow, he felt lucky that day. Without hesitation, he went out to the North Hollywood station parking lot and grabbed one of the 'dick cars.'

He headed for South-Central in hopes that the van would reappear. This time he slowly drove down 47th Street hoping to have better luck. To his surprise there was a dirty brown utility van parked directly in front of the house listed on the gas bill. Even though it was mid-April, he felt it was like Christmas had arrived early and he had been given a gift that would continue to go on giving.

Since the witness, Sally Talles, didn't get a license number, the detective had only a description. This vehicle parked in front of the residence was definitely brown in color and could be described as a utility van. Further it had the earmark of being the type of vehicle the witness had described. But the detective needed some way of identifying this as the van that the shooter got into.

He remembered how the witness had difficulty describing the condition of the van. She alluded to the fact there was some type of covering on one of the windows. She had claimed it was some type of white paper or plastic glued or taped to one of the van's side windows. In order to better view the windows of this parked van, he got out of his 'Crown Vic' and walked around the exterior of the van. He tried to act as nonchalant as possible hoping no one would tip off the owner of the van.

When the detective walked out into the street, he could get a better look at the side window of the van. The one window seemed to be covered with a cardboard of some type held in place by duct tape. Could this be what witness Sally was trying to describe? The only way to find out was to take a photo of it and show it to this witness. The detective headed back to his car and picked up a camera. He got into their car and had the other detective drive by the van. The detective with the camera continued to click a number of photos as they drove by.

Without any further ado they headed back to North Hollywood station so he could print out some copies of his photos. When that was done, he contacted witness Talles to see when she would be able to look at the photos of the van.

Arrangements were made and in short order he showed the photos to the witness. Detective Kirby handed her a stack of photographs and asked her to review them. She said apologetically, "I don't think I can be of any help since I didn't get the license number of the van." He replied, "I understand but could you please look over these photos."

This was such a critical moment for the detective. He knew this was a long shot since this witness had told him more than a week ago that she was scared to death. Then she had related to him that her main concern was hoping that the shooters didn't see her trying to hide behind her father's pickup truck. The detective was fixated on Sally's eyes hoping to see if she showed any sign of recognizing the van.

All of a sudden Sally's pensive look turn to a slight smile as her face seemed to light up. She hesitated for words to express her shock and amazement. As her finger pointed to one of the photos her mouth shouted out the words, "THAT'S THE VAN, I SAW!"

Those were the greatest set of words the detective had heard in a long time. He didn't want to be disappointed but he wanted to be sure that Sally was certain as to her identification of the van. He uttered the words, "Are you sure that was the van you saw that night?" She turned to the detective and said, "Yea, that's it." She took her index finger and started pointing to the photo of the vans covered-up window. "That's the window I told you about that had some type of cardboard or plastic covering it." She went on saying, "That's the van I'm sure of it. Look, it is a dark brown just how I described it."

Detective Kirby expressed his appreciation to Sally and thanked her for making time for him to show her the photos. As he turned away, he tried his best not to show his exuberance. He tried to contain his emotions since Homicide Detectives are not supposed to show their human feelings. He wanted to shout, "Hallelujah." (His real words were most likely a little bit stronger.)

As elated as he was, he knew that his investigative work had just begun. First, he needed to take the license plate number of the van he had written down and run it through DMV to find out who was the registered owner. His hope was that RO would magically be the killer and he would be able close the case as SOLVED. But most clues don't lead directly to the killer but only open doors to further investigation.

Back at the station, he entered the license plate number FAR325 into the DMV system and received a surprising response. The RO was listed as a Juan Garcia with an address of 726 West 81st Street in South-Central Los Angeles. The detective had rejected the idea that the person listed on the gas bill, Cecil Avila, was the shooter because Sally had described the shooter as being a person who was built like a male. But this Juan Garcia could be the shooter although his age seemed older than the person Sally had described. The detective decided that he needed to follow up on the information about the van.

After a discussion with his boss, Detective Carson, it was decided to find out more about who was the real person who was using this brown van. This time Detective Kirby was accompanied by his boss and they went to the address in South-Central LA listed on the gas bill. Detective Kirby felt a special urgency since the eyewitness had been able to identify the van. He and his boss pulled up near the house in question but the van was gone.

Detective Kirby had to think that when he originally checked out the brown van maybe the owner or user of the van saw him nosing around. This may have caused that person to move the van and hide it. The detectives decided to sit and wait to see if the van returned. After an hour surveilling the location, they decided to check out some other locations in the area. As they left the site, Detective Kirby began second-guessing his original decision of not seizing the van earlier. He had to wonder if he had let the best evidence slip away right under his nose?

An hour later when they returned the detectives saw the old brown van parked next to the curb in front of the house. Detective Kirby couldn't get the words out of his mouth fast enough, "Thank God it is here." At that moment the tough-minded detective was a true believer in the Easter Bunny and Santa Claus. From that moment on, LAPD kept 24-hour surveillance on the van until they were ready to seize it. A special team of surveillance detectives were placed in strategic places on the street to observe the old van at all times.

CHAPTER 10 – SO MANY LOOSE ENDS

At various times during the early morning hours when no one was around, the detectives had the opportunity to check out this van. When they were able to glance inside the windows, they saw a totally delipidated vehicle. The front seats were torn and worn bare thin. The dashboard had been partially ripped out where a car radio had been. The steering wheel was missing the horn section that once contained an airbag.

The van's headliner had been replaced with red cloth with a pink fringe hanging down above the windshield. This certainly could be a sign of pride of ownership.

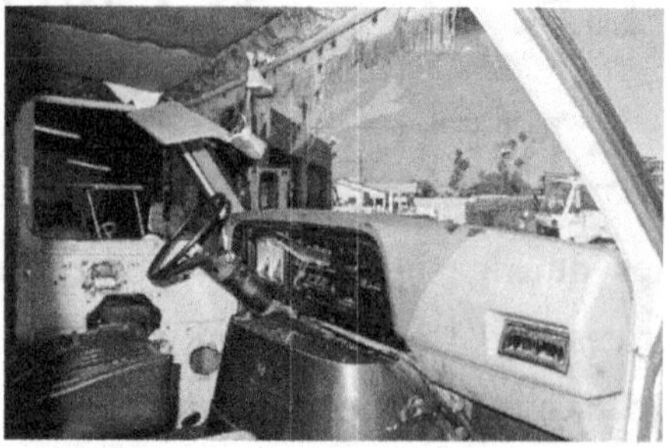

The interior of the van had been someone's delight since there was evidence that the doors and walls had been covered with some type of wood paneling. It might have had a splendid look when installed but over the years it had been neglected. Someone had gone to considerable trouble installing blue shag carpet throughout the entire van's floor. The middle row of seats had been removed so there would be sufficient room for a mattress. To some, a lumpy soiled mattress may have created a somewhat of a romantic atmosphere especially after dark.

The van had all the markings of a 'pimpmobile' that had lost its sensuous appeal over time. Now it could be described as a utility van on its last leg. However, it might be more accurately described as a 'Bucket of Bolts' ready for the wrecking yard compactor. No matter how unattractive this van might seem, the detectives were hoping that this van would be the key to solving this conspiracy to Murder.

The detectives made contact with the registered owner Juan Garcia who admitted that he had owned the van for some time. He indicated that something was wrong with the power steering and he constantly had to add fluid to the power steering reservoir. Also, there was some type of water leak either from the radiator or one of the hoses. Constantly he was having to fill the radiator every time he wanted to use it. Because of all the problems, he didn't use it that much anymore because it was not very reliable. He had given the van to his step-son, Wilson Sanchez, to drive around the neighborhood.

Then the detectives focused on the date of April 9th and asked Juan if he was using it at that time. Juan thought for a moment and shook his head saying, "I haven't used it for several months. The only person using that old van on that date would be my step-son Wilson Sanchez."

At that point in time the detectives felt that they were onto something in that they had a strong belief that they knew who was the primary user of the van. Also, the surveillance team kept seeing a young Hispanic male driving the van for short distances.

At the same time the detectives wished to make contact with the Mrs. Cecilia Avila at 202 East 47th Street. They wanted to ask her how her gas bill end up on a street, miles away in the San Fernando Valley. Also, they wanted to inquire what she knew about an old brown van parked along the street in front of her house.

With that new intriguing information, they decided to head over to 47th Street to have a talk with this Cecilia Avila. When they arrived at her place, they rang the doorbell and waited. Shortly they heard a woman's voice from behind the front door. In a curt voice she said, "What do you want?" She wasn't about to open her door to any stranger. The detectives tried to muster up a pleasant greeting by saying, "This is the police and we would like to talk to a 'Cecilia Avila.'" All they could hear was the woman say, "What did you say?"

The detectives wondered whether she was just a frightened resident afraid of strangers or was she purposely trying to be uncooperative with the police. The detectives tried to assure her that they weren't out to get her but only wanted to talk to her for a minute. Apparently, the detective's congenial greeting got her to open the door. They said, "Could we come in and talk to you about your gas bill?"

She hesitated for a moment and Detective Kirby pulled out of his notebook a copy of the gas bill. She said, "Okay come on in. Can I see what you have there?" The detectives stepped into the house. Kirby handed the copy of the gas bill to her. With a surprised expression she gazed at the piece of paper and said, "Where did you get this?" The detectives didn't want to say too much and asked again, "Is it your gas company bill?" With a look of disbelief on her face, she said, "I paid that gas bill, I know I did."

The detective realized that she was misunderstanding the reason why they were showing her the bill. He said, "We're not concerned about whether you paid this gas bill but if you could explain how this gas bill ended up in the street in Sun Valley?" She replied, "Where is Sun Valley?" It became apparent that she had no idea where Sun Valley was and continually shook her head.

She was totally perplexed. Putting on her glasses in order to better study the gas bill, she related that it looked like a copy of one of her gas bills. She went on to explain that she pays the bills each month and places the receipt of the bill in a box in the kitchen. She went on the defensive. She raised her voice in indignation that the police would try to say that she didn't pay her bills on time. The detective again tried to calm her down and assured her that they weren't implying that the bill hadn't been paid. He went on to ask if anyone else would handle her gas bills.

Cecilia sat in the chair with a blank look that soon turned to a pensive look. She asked the detective if he meant the gas bill that her daughter had borrowed to give to Wilson Sanchez. She quickly added that he needed it to obtain a 'Library Card.'

In order to acquire a library card, a person had to prove that he had a permanent address. The reason for that requirement was to provide a means of tracking down library books which haven't been returned on time. The detective was trying to grasp what she had just said. Since he had a confused look on his face about what she had said, she looked directly at the detective and told him the facts about living in the barrio.

They asked about this person she called Wilson Sanchez since they had heard that name before from the register owner of the van. She exclaimed that he was her daughter's boyfriend. Over the past several months he had moved into her daughter's bedroom. She went on to say that he drove an old brown van which he often parked in front of the house.

The detectives next question was whether Wilson gave her back that gas bill? She replied she didn't remember him giving it back to her. She agreed to check her stack of gas bill receipts. Later she informed the detective that she had searched for that gas bill and couldn't locate it. She assumed that Wilson had never returned it.

CHAPTER 11- PULLING OVER THE VAN

The detectives notified the surveillance team to make contact with the parties the next time they saw the van being used. Several days later the surveillance team followed the van that had two occupants in it as it pulled up to the house in question. The one officer approached the driver and asked for his identification. The driver showed him some ID with the name Wilson Sanchez. The driver explained that he didn't have his driver's license on him. When asked whose van this was, the driver admitted that it was his although the registration was in his stepfather's name. He explained that his stepfather didn't need it so he had been using it full-time for several months.

When the detectives started talking about the old van, he had no problems admitting he was the primary user of it. When they asked about his using it several weeks ago in particular April 9th, he admitted to being the user.

When Wilson was asked for his address where he lived, he hesitated and said, "It all depends. I used to stay with my stepdad but lately I have been living with my girlfriend at her place." He went on to say her name was Amy Avila (pseudonym) and her address was 202 E. 47th Street. The driver pointed to the house several car lengths in front of them and said, "That's the place."

He was further asked if his girlfriend's mother was Cecilia Avila, to which the driver nodded in the affirmative. Wilson Sanchez had a puzzled look on his face. He was thinking how do they know his girlfriend's mother's name as Cecilia Avila.

At that moment in time Wilson had to start doing some creative thinking as to how to explain the van being driven all the way out in the San Fernando Valley. He didn't want to get his buddies Erik and Pablo involved.

Another detective had gone to the passenger side of the van and asked for identification. This passenger handed the detective some form of identification with the name Pablo Alvarenga.

The detective talked briefly to both Wilson Sanchez and Pablo Alvarenga hoping to learn more information about the use of the van. At that stage the detectives had a lot of loose ends but they didn't want to arrest anyone until they had additional evidence.

CHAPTER 12- WHAT WAS WIFE'S ROLE?

The detectives were certain they had tracked down the van that was used in the shooting. Exactly who was driving it and who did the shooting were still unanswered questions. No one had to remind the detectives that you can't prosecute a van. They needed to find out what individuals were involved. The most perplexing part of the case was the wife whose statements and reactions to her husband's death didn't pass the smell taste.

This shooting had the earmarks of a Domestic Violence (DV) case especially when the wife showed no emotion about her husband being shot. She claimed she didn't hear the gunshots or the responding emergency vehicles. Most of all she claimed that she knew that her husband was having an affair with another woman. However, the facts didn't seem to prove that she shot her husband. According to witness Sally Talles, the wife didn't fit the description of the person seen running from the crime scene to the van. There were more questions that needed to be answered.

Just days after the shooting Detective Kirby swung by the house to talk to the wife. At that time, he was concerned that it might be considered insensitive to ask certain personal questions. He needed some answers in order to know how to proceed with the investigation. He tried to delicately asked her questions about life insurance. Just asking such a cold question to a person who had just become a widow less than 24 hours earlier might be considered as crass and unsympathetic. The detective thought he could sugar coat the question by asking if she was going to be able to afford a funeral. Then he would slip in the question whether she had life insurance benefits to cover the costs.

His diplomacy apparently worked since she had no difficulty talking about the Primerica Life Insurance policy for $225,000 that the couple had taken out on each other's lives. She freely admitted that they were having financial problems and were considering declaring bankruptcy. She claimed this was due to an identity thief that had cost them $87,000. It wasn't hard to see how that all fit together.

The detective was trying to gently waltz around the issue of the stability of the marriage. She didn't try to hide the fact that she knew that her husband was having an affair with a younger woman. She even mentioned that she had considered divorcing her husband, Reynaldo, and discussed it with her son Tony Herrera.

After the interview the detective wanted to evaluate all of this new information about the life insurance, the discussion of a divorce, and possible bankruptcy. The detective needed to pin the wife down as to what she was doing specifically on the day of the homicide. The best way to do that was to obtain her cellphone records which would show who she had been in contact with. The detective prepared a search warrant for her phone records.

When he received the package of records from the phone company, he made a cursory review of calls leading up to the shooting. He couldn't believe all the calls that she had made to one specific phone number. What surprised him most was all the calls that had been made during the period she claimed she was asleep. Something wasn't computing quite right. Either she had given her phone to someone else or she had been lying about going to sleep shortly after 8:00 p.m.

As much as the detective didn't want to be so suspicious of a recent widow, he knew it was time to have a heart to heart talk with the wife. This time he wanted it to be at the police station so he could tape the interview. On April 18th he was able to reach her by phone and asked her if she could come by the station the next day.

During that phone conversation the wife made a strange comment to the detective that aroused his suspicions even more. She mentioned that her husband's father now was looking at her like she was the person who killed his son. Her response to the father was, "If you think that I killed him you had better have proof. I was home when he was killed." The detective interpreted that to mean that others beside the police had some skepticism about the wife's story.

After the detective had reviewed the wife's phone activity, he noticed an inordinate number of phone calls to one particular phone number (323) 804-7768. As a result, the detective obtained a search warrant for that number. It came back registered to a Frank Ramos (Pseudonym) who lived on Cherokee Ave, in Los Angeles. That wasn't anywhere near to the address on the gas bill and certainly was nowhere near the scene of the crime. The detectives checked that name through the police records and didn't find any criminal record under that name. This Mr. Ramos seem to be squeaky clean and not the type to be involved in a Murder.

The detective didn't want to blow the cover of the investigation by contacting Mr. Ramos, but the detectives needed to know why was the wife calling and receiving calls from that particular cellphone number. Could the wife have been having an affair with this Mr. Ramos? Or could she have had some type of business with him? The detective didn't have time to waste merely speculating the reason for so many phone calls.

Time was running out for the scheduled meeting the detectives had set up with the wife. The detective contacted Mr. Ramos and asked him about all the calls on his cellphone number (323) 804-7768. To the detective's surprise the conversation was highly revealing. Mr. Ramos denied making any of those calls. He claimed that he didn't even have such a phone number.

At that point the detective read to him from the phone records that his name was listed as the registered owner of that number. There was a dead silence on the line for several seconds. Then Mr. Ramos replied that must be the cellphone he purchased for a distant relative who couldn't get a phone because of bad credit history. The detective wondered if this Mr. Ramos was shining him on. The detective asked directly who did he give this cellphone to. Again, there was hesitancy from Mr. Ramos. He tried to explain that he didn't want to have any trouble with the phone company for fraudulently getting the phone for a poverty-stricken relative.

The detective smiled to himself thinking this guy was so afraid of the phone company, when the detective was trying to nail someone on a homicide. Now, the detective was trying to reassure Mr. Ramos that he wasn't going to get into trouble for falsely obtaining a phone in his name for someone else.

After a lengthy period of silence and reflection Mr. Ramos said, "I got it for Oscar Rene Alvarado. Is he in trouble for not paying the phone company? If so, I am sorry and I will pay the amount for him." The detective didn't know how to respond since Mr. Ramos sounded sincere but the jaded detective had misjudged people on prior occasions. The detective responded by asking for an address for this Mr. Alvarado. Mr. Ramos said he didn't have a complete address but thought it was somewhere on 84nd Street in LA. At that point the detective said thanks for the information and they would get back with him if they needed anything more.

The detective looked at his watch and saw that he had to get all his paperwork together before the meeting with the wife. Fifteen minutes later he received the word from the front desk that the wife, Maria Quijano, was waiting for him. The North Hollywood LAPD station had several so-called

'Interrogation rooms' which the public are told are 'Interview rooms.' Detective Kirby had to see which room wasn't in use.

He found that one of the rooms appeared to be vacant, so he walked in and plunked down his police reports. Then he hurriedly went to the lobby and met Maria. After a brief salutation he escorted her to the interview room and told her to have a seat and make herself comfortable. Before he could ask his first question, she indicated that she wanted to use the lady's room. Without missing a beat, he stood up and said, "That's a good idea before we get started." He walked her to the area of the restroom and pointed to the women's room. While standing waiting for her to finish, he stepped over to the front counter where the station had a coffee urn. He poured a cup of black coffee which looked dark black and had the odor that it had been sitting around for hours. The detective smiled to himself that it would have to do since he didn't have time to drive to the local Starbucks to have a fresh venti cup of coffee.

CHAPTER 13- MARIA'S STATEMENTS BEFORE ARREST

When the wife came out of the restroom, she was escorted back to the interview room. She could see Detective Kirby had a cup of coffee. In order to project a pleasant atmosphere, he immediately said, "Would you like some coffee before we begin?" She looked at his steely black coffee that looked like one needed a knife to cut through it. She instantly responded, "No thanks, I am fine."

Both sat down and little did Maria know that she was about to seal her fate for the rest of her life on what she was about to say. The first questioning was like going down memory lane with her husband and herself. She was asked again about her relationship with her husband. Once more she maintained that she was treated like a queen by her husband. But when asked about her suspicions that her husband was having an affair, she agreed that she didn't like that. She even admitted that they had considered a divorce but for some unknown reason she claimed that everything was fine.

In her next breath she said that she believed that her husband was murdered because of his girlfriend and his mistakes. That was followed by her saying that her husband was a loving and good father. When asked details about the date of the Murder, she maintained that she didn't hear the gunshots or the sirens. Yet she admitted that she might have heard her husband coming home from work, although she didn't see him. She repeated that his routine was to grab a slice of bread and glass of milk from the kitchen and retreat into the bedroom.

The questions up to this point weren't confrontational. Then the detective eased into the subject about the life insurance. He asked for more specifics about the life insurance policy. She didn't hesitate to explain that she had contacted the Primerica Insurance Company about how to submit a claim. Then the detective asked if she had told her husband's relatives about the life insurance policy. She hesitated for a moment before answering. Eventually she admitted that she had told them that her husband never had an insurance policy.

Then the detective switched the topic to the bank records of the victim. Again, she delayed in answering. After a pregnant pause she hastily responded that it was none of their business. She went on claiming that her husband's father was more than a pain in the ass. He was sticking his nose in their family business. The detective could quickly sense there was some bad blood between her and the in-laws.

Then the detective wanted to move on to another subject but didn't want to irritate her so much that she would refuse to continue to talk. He asked if she was familiar with an **Oscar Alvarado**. How was she going to react? At first, she pretended that she hadn't heard the name. Her mind was spinning like a top about to whirl off a table. What should she say? She wanted to appear calm and composed.

The detective reiterated the name "Oscar Alvarado." "Who is he?" Again, there was another protracted silence. At that point, the detective revealed another unexpected fact. He clarified by saying that he noticed that she had called an Oscar Alvarado shortly before her husband's death. She leaned back in her chair almost to the point of tipping over. She caught herself before falling. Her mind was racing so rapidly that she almost passed out.

At this moment in time she knew that she had to collect her thoughts if she wanted to outsmart the detective. Now she knew that the detective had information about the use of her cellphone. To explain why she would have contact with this guy Alvarado, she quickly replied by saying that he was the father of a person who had rented a room from them several months ago.

She went on with her story that this young person owed rent money and his father Mr. Alvarado had called her about paying off this debt of his son's. She felt that she had dodged the bullet since that would explain why Mr. Alvarado and she had phone calls to each other. With a sigh of relief, she felt self-confidence that she had covered her ass.

Without any warning the detective dropped the second shoe that would box her in forever. The detective glanced at the phone records in front of him. He picked up one page and handed it over to her. As she was glancing at it, he said, "How do you explain over 18 calls to Mr. Alvarado?" She tried to avoid answering the detective by continuing to gaze at the phone record in her hand.

After the detective gave her time to respond, he asked whether Mr. Alvarado had come over to her house on the night of the shooting to pay off the rent owed by his son. To that question Maria tried to deflect any personal contact between Alvarado and herself. She seemed to want to wash her hands of any contact with him. At no time did she say anything about Mr. Alvarado committing any harm to her husband.

The detective said he wanted to review the facts with her. The detective said that he recalled her saying that she had fallen asleep around 8:00 p.m. the night of the shooting. In the most diplomatic voice he could summons up, he asked how come there were all these phone calls after 8:00 p.m.? All Maria could do was make a facial expression of being surprised. All she could say was that maybe she was wrong about the time she went to sleep.

The interview was coming to an end as Maria gave vague answers to the detective. At some point it became clear that nothing useful was being elicited from further questioning. Detective Kirby thanked Maria for coming in and said he would get back to her if he had any more follow-up questions. Maria slowly rose up from the battered interrogation chair and leaned over to pick up her purse from the floor. As she walked out of the interrogation room, she appeared to be in some type of bewilderment.

Did she say the right thing or did she say something that would incriminate her? As she continued to walk to the lobby of the police station no one was stopping and arresting her. By the time she got outside she took a deep breath. She thought to herself that she must have said the right thing because she was outside the police jail and seemed to be as free as a bird.

The detective knew that Maria wasn't being candid. Her story didn't compute. But how did the van located in South-Central LA connect with her? What was most troubling was, how did this guy Alvarado factor into the killing? Over the next nine days they needed to pull all the loose ends together.

CHAPTER 14 SEARCH WARRANT TIME

Now with the plethora of information that they had received from Cecilia Arias, the gas bill lady; Juan Garcia, the stepfather; Frank Ramos the cellphone purchaser; and the surveillance team, the detectives decided to prepare search warrants for various locations. The hope was that the searches might reveal some incriminating evidence that would result in arrests being made.

The detectives recognized that it was crucial that all the searches occur at the same time. The purpose was to prevent the first group of suspects from tipping off the others so they couldn't destroy evidence.

Some 19 days after the shooting, the detectives prepared their search warrants to be presented to a judge. Even though it required extensive time and resources of the detective bureau, the detectives wanted everything to be properly done so the evidence recovered couldn't be thrown out on a legal technicality. Having a judge to review and approve the warrants would help in the prosecution of the case when it came time for trial.

It was early in the morning when a crew of detectives left North Hollywood station to execute the search warrants in South-Central. As they drove through Hollywood the sun was barely coming up. At this time of the morning Tinseltown didn't look all that glamorous without all its glittering lights on. Traffic was light as they cruised down the Hollywood Freeway and passed over sacred ground for LAPD. As their vehicles passed over the

Gower Street freeway bridge, they could look down to their right and see the tall steeple of Hollywood Presbyterian Church.

Just across the street they could make out the intersection of Gower Street and Carlos Street. That was where law enforcement history was made. Back in 1963, two LAPD officers assigned to the undercover robbery detail pulled over two suspects at that intersection. During this traffic stop the one suspect was able to pull a gun on Officer Campbell as they walked to the curb. The suspect with the gun ordered the other Officer Hettinger to hand over his gun or his partner would be shot. Officer Hettinger recognized that his partner was in danger of being shot so he begrudgingly handed over his service revolver.

Afterwards the suspects drove the officers to the onion fields of Bakersfield, California, where Suspect Powell shot Officer Campbell. Fortunately, Officer Hettinger was able to escape; however, he was forever vilified by the LAPD administration for giving up his weapon. After Officer Campbell's death all the new cadets going through the Police Academy were taught, 'Never give up your weapon.'

None of the detectives cruising over this site said a word to each other. But each one of them had to think to themselves what would they do if they were ever faced with the situation that Officer Hettinger found himself in. These were the tough decisions that none of these detectives wanted to face that morning in executing these search warrants.

As to the first two search warrants, they were directed to the locations where Wilson Sanchez lived. One was for Cecilia Avila's house at 202 E. 47nd Street, Los Angeles where he now lived with Amy who was Cecilia's daughter. The detectives wanted to look through Cecilia's stack of gas bills. But most of all they were hoping maybe they could find the handgun used to shoot the victim. If not the gun, maybe they might find expended shell casings that could be compared to the ones recovered at the crime scene. Unfortunately, the search revealed few useful items except for other gas bills for that address and evidence showing that Wilson Sanchez was living at that location.

The other location involving Wilson was that of his stepfather's place where he previously lived. Again, this search didn't turn up much except for the papers showing the stepfather owned the old brown Ford van.

The next search warrant involved Oscar Alvarado's place. It was for his apartment at 939 W 84th Street, Los Angeles, where the detectives hoped to find evidence showing he knew or had contact with Maria. At this stage the detectives thought that Alvarado may have been the actual shooter, so they also were hoping to find the handgun that had been used. The other item they wanted to recover was the cellphone he used to contact Maria. The result of the search didn't yield any handgun but it did result in the recovery of the cellphone.

Another search warrant concerning the cellphone involved Mr. Ramos who was the person who had purchased that cellphone for Oscar Alvarado. At that location the detectives obtained the registration papers for the phone from Mr. Ramos who was very cooperative. All he had intended to do was to help out a relative who couldn't get the phone because he had bad credit. He was more than shocked that he ended up as a suspect in a Murder investigation, especially since he could better be described as a 'law and order' type.

The remaining search warrant affected Maria's house at 737 Arcola, Sun Valley. The detectives were hoping to find some items or documents that connected her to Mr. Alvarado. The only items they found were papers that showed that Alvarado used Maria's address on some type of medical records.

While conducting the search warrants the detectives at the same time arrested Maria Quijano, Oscar Alvarado and Wilson Sanchez. The detectives wanted to talk to each one of them. They especially wanted to further discuss with Maria why so many things she had stated didn't seem to add up. What was most revealing was when they arrested Oscar Alvarado it became apparent that he was considerably older than all the others. He was in fact 59 years old. They noticed that he had difficulty walking. As they lead him to the police car, he seemed to drag his left foot and when he put pressure on it, he limped to the side.

Since detectives are suspicious by nature, they started to wonder how could Alvarado have shot the victim and run all that distance to the getaway van. The more they watched Alvarado as he went through the booking procedure, the more they started to doubt the claim that it was Alvarado who did the shooting. If Alvarado wasn't physically able to run to the van, then who was the real shooter? It was clear that it was time to again talk to Wilson Sanchez.

By now the detectives had a number of questions to ask Wilson not only about the van but what happened regarding the gas bill he borrowed from his girlfriend's mom.

The detectives were amazed that Wilson was able to drive this old Ford Econoline utility van all the way to the San Fernando Valley and back twice without it breaking down. Either he was an extremely lucky person or it was a great testimonial to the durability of **Ford Econoline Utility Vans**.

CHAPTER 15 STATEMENTS AFTER ARREST

Not until April 28, 2005, did the police attempt to interview Maria Quijano again. That was the date when the detectives carried out multiple search warrants on the various locations. In the process Maria was picked up and brought to the station. There Detective Kirby sat her down in another one of the interview rooms at the police station. By now she most likely was beginning to feel the walls closing in on her. The detective told her she needed to tell the true and the full story as to what happened before it was too late. He explained that parts of her story didn't make sense. She had the look of a woman who was over her head in lies and about to drown. She was looking for someone to throw her a life saver.

This time the detective was much more direct when asking her questions. He opened by asking about her relationship with her husband. Instead of saying that everything was fine, this time she emphasized that she was angry with Reynaldo and was jealous of his affair with the other woman. She even admitted that he had asked her for a divorce twice. However, since Reynaldo was paying for everything, she didn't want a divorce which would end all of this support.

When asked in a hypothetical fashion if she killed her husband her answer was not what the detective was expecting. She said, "If I were going to kill my husband, I would had done it at his work." The detective found her answer to be uncanny. But then she proceeded to say, "I swear I didn't plan anything."

Next Detective Kirby tried to focus on her claim that she was asleep throughout the shooting. Since she knew the detectives had obtained the phone records, she changed her response accordingly. Now she said that she was awake and did use her cellphone. But she continued to deny that she heard the shooting or sirens.

When directly asked how many calls she made to Alvarado, she tried to keep her answer vague. That may have been because she really couldn't recall all the calls that were made between the two of them. When pressed she said maybe there were three or four calls between us.

The interview lasted longer than expected when the tape recorder indicated it was at the end of the tape. This might have been the perfect time to take a break but the detectives were on a roll and weren't going to let this opportunity escape their grasp. The one detective grabbed another blank tape from the drawer and without any delay inserted it in the recorder.

Kirby said to Maria, "Where were we?" Followed by, "Okay let's go back to where you were talking about a divorce. Why didn't you want a divorce?" Maria fidget in the old rickety interrogation chair as though she was uncomfortable with that line of questioning. Pausing for a moment, she appeared to be trying to collect her thoughts. Then she shocked the detective by saying, "I should have divorced Reynaldo before it went too far." As though she realized that she may have let the cat out of the bag she immediately stated, "I swear I never planned to do anything wrong to my husband."

She seemed to want to explain that she was the real victim in the situation. She wanted to insert her husband's girlfriend into the discussion. She said, "I wish he would have spent more time with me instead of her." By this time Maria must have known that she hadn't been consistent in her story. When the detective asked her if she had been truthful in what she had told the police on the day of the shooting, Maria now put her head down on the table in a contrite manner.

Apologetically she stated that she hadn't been totally truthful. She was sorry but now she was willing to tell the truth. Then she admitted that she had a conversation with Mr. Alvarado around 10:30 p.m. Next, she volunteered that she was a light sleeper but still didn't hear anything. The interview ended by her stating unequivocally, "I swear to God. I didn't send him outside."

Since now she was under arrest and in custody, the detective led her over to the holding cell and told her that he had someone he wanted her to talk to about the matter. He didn't know whether he could set it up with such short notice, but he would get back with her.

CHAPTER 16-TIME FOR THE RUSE

Detective Kirby made a few calls and was able to track down Edward Younger (Pseudonym). He was a special interrogator who had refined his interrogation skills. He was now retired but LAPD would contract with him to help interrogate various subjects in problematical cases. At 7:30 a.m. Maria was brought out of the holding celling where she had spent the night. Since she hadn't ever spent a night in jail before, this had been an unsettling experience for her.

She was brought over to one of the other interrogation rooms and took a seat. Within minutes Edward Younger came in and introduced himself to her. He explained that he had been asked by Detective Kirby to talk to her to see what really happened to her husband. He cordially started out to see if she was all right and said, "Are you okay or do you need anything." She looked up at him and requested if she could use the restroom. Younger, who was still standing in front of her, told her to come with him.

She stood up and stepped out of the tiny room. She followed him out where he found a female staff member to escort her to the restroom. After a ten-minute delay Maria was brought back to the interrogation room. Younger started out by engaging in small talk to gain a sympathetic rapport with Maria. He didn't want to seem confrontational or even judgmental.

He realized that Maria wanted to paint an image that she was the victim. She went on about all the lies her husband had told her over the years to cover his affair. She should have gone along with the divorce and terminated the troubled marriage. Yet what bothered her most was the fact that earlier her husband had taken advantage of her daughter. She went into more detail claiming that he had raped her daughter when she was little.

Younger seized on this revolution by saying, "That must have been terrible for you." He explained that he couldn't blame her for what she did. He emphasized that no mother would tolerate such vile acts by her husband. The interrogator planted the seed that it was okay to do bad things to her wayward and wicked husband.

Younger said that he knew that she had planned harm to come to her husband with the help of Mr. Alvarado. Although the interrogator didn't have any actual evidence of such a fact, he wanted to see what would be Maria's reaction. The interrogator was correct in that Maria didn't deny having plans with Alvarado to harm Reynaldo. As a matter of fact, Maria explained that she had begun planning harm to her husband as far back as four to six months earlier. She had discussed with Alvarado the various possibilities of things that could happen to her 'no-good' husband.

For some reason Maria wanted to explain how upset she was with her husband. She related that Alvarado had told her that to kill her husband would cost her somewhere between $20,000 to $25,000. She explained that she didn't have that type of money. She related that the people wanted their money upfront. Maria lamented that the only way she could pay such a large amount was from the life insurance proceeds which she wouldn't receive until much later. The hitmen didn't want to wait but wanted their money up front.

When Younger heard that, he said that would mean that your husband would have to die in order to collect the life insurance money. She may not have understood the ramifications of what she had just said. Then she folded her arms tightly and emphatically said, "I didn't want death in my house."

Younger didn't know how to construe her response. He asked if that meant that she really didn't want to kill him but really wanted to teach him a lesson? She seemed to grasp the idea that she only wanted Alvarado to beat up her husband. When pressed by Younger, she acknowledged that she understood that such a beating could result in death.

She explained that she had agreed to pay $800 (this is the amount she would pay for a beating) for someone to beat up her husband but she wasn't paying anyone to kill her husband. At that point, Younger leaned back in his chair and with a sympathetic voice volunteered, "Did they go too far?" Without any encouragement she picked up the hint and said, "I just wanted them to scare him or something. Somehow they went too far and killed him."

Since all the statements had been tape-recorded, Younger felt that he had been successful in getting Maria to open up about her involvement in her husband's death. He stood up and excused himself as she sat all alone in this sterile interrogation room. He walked away from the interrogating area and proceeded to the detectives in the bureau. He shook his head and exclaimed that she wouldn't admit to killing her husband. The most she would admit to was that she wanted someone to beat up her husband. He directed the other detectives to go in and talk to her about the specifics of what she was now saying.

Both detectives Thompson and Haines entered the interrogation room explaining that they needed a truthful statement from her in order to fill out their police reports.

CHAPTER 17- WILSON SANCHEZ COMES CLEAN

When the detectives got all the arrestees booked and all the items recovered from the search warrants placed in the evidence locker, it was time to have a little chat with Wilson Sanchez. They advised Wilson of his Miranda Rights and explained that they would like to talk to him to clarify Alvarado's involvement of doing the shooting. Wilson was thinking maybe he could talk his way out of the situation so he agreed to waive his rights and talk.

Originally Wilson tried to say that he had loaned his van to Mr. Alvarado who used it for a job. Then he changed his story indicating that he may have gone with the old guy, Alvarado, but he had no idea what he was going to do. With this explanation his fellow hitmen wouldn't be mentioned so they would be spared. Wilson claimed that he didn't know that it was going to be a shooting until Alvarado ran back to the van with the gun. At first Wilson must have thought the detectives were buying his story.

Little did he know that the detectives had an eyewitness who saw the **shooter running**. Since Alvarado was elderly and had a distinct limp when he walked, there was no way Alvarado could have done that running after the shooting.

Wilson reiterated that it was Alvarado's idea and he was the one who drove to the location and he got out and did the shooting and ran back and got in the van. The detective in a non-confrontational way told Wilson that was impossible since Alvarado walked with a severe limp. Wilson sat in the chair like a reindeer looking at an oncoming car. He didn't know how to react.

Should he stop talking or should he come up with another story? Wilson wasn't the sharpest knife in the drawer. This time he said that the guy had to be shot since he had raped a little girl. He tried to justify the shooting but he wasn't explaining who really did the shooting. When the detectives pressed him, he answered as though he had done a noble thing in shooting the sexual pervert. The detective wasn't certain he heard Wilson right.

In order to flush out the details, the detective tried to go over the shooting scenario. Then the shooter of the rapist, was you? Wilson nodded his head and wanted to list all the reasons the shooting was done. He didn't seem to realize that he was admitting to doing the shooting but somehow, he wanted the detective to know it was justified in killing the evil victim.

At this point he changed his story. Now his tale was that he and a friend Pablo Alvarenga drove out to the house in the San Fernando Valley. They waited for the bad guy to come out and that was when he got out of the van and ran up to the car and did the shooting. He ran back to the van and his friend Alvarenga drove back to South-Central.

When asked about Oscar Alvarado being involved, he waited a few moments to regroup his thoughts. Then he explained that Alvarado only gave them a photo of the bad guy and the address explaining how to get there. The detectives knew that Maria had been calling Oscar Alvarado's cellphone minutes before the shooting and shortly thereafter. Wilson's new story wasn't explaining all the contact between Maria and Oscar Alvarado. The detectives continued to listen to Wilson digging a deeper hole for himself in which he would never be able to climb out of.

CHAPTER 18 WHAT WAS OSCAR ALVARADO'S STORY?

When the detectives found that Maria's cellphone had called and received numerous phone calls from a phone number (323) 804-7768 they checked that number out. As stated earlier that cellphone was registered to a Frank Ramos who when contacted explained that he got the phone for a Mr. Rene Oscar Serrano Alvarado who lived at 939 W. 84th Street in South-Central Los Angeles. When Mr. Alvarado was contacted, he admitted having such a cellphone and making several calls on it on April 9th. However, he was vague as to who he might have called that night.

On April 28, 2005, one of the search warrants was for his apartment where the cellphone (323) 804-7768 was found and seized as evidence. Mr. Alvarado was arrested and transported to the North Hollywood Division station. The detectives had talked to Maria Quijano and Wilson Sanchez, and finally got around to talking to Mr. Alvarado. Wilson had been arrested on prior occasions so he knew the drill of being booked with all the fingerprinting and booking photos.

Yet for Mr. Alvarado this was all new to him. Even though he was the oldest suspect, he was a complete neophyte as to what to expect. The detectives wanted each of the suspects to think that their co-conspirators had talked to the police earlier. So, the detectives went out of their way to make sure that Alvarado saw that Wilson and Maria were both being interviewed by other detectives. In that way the detectives planted the idea that their companions had implicated them.

The detectives commenced their interrogation of Alvarado in a congenial way. First by asking if he was doing okay. Or if he needed something. Mr. Alvarado had to be suspicious of the situation but he was grasping on to any kindhearted words coming his way. The detectives stated that they wanted to get his side of the story but first they needed to advise him of his Miranda Rights. He listened carefully to what they had to say and he exhibited an eagerness to tell his story.

He responded that he wanted to waive his right to an attorney wanted to talk to them. The detectives started asking a series of questions. They again asked him if he lived at 9039 West 84th Street to which he nodded his head and said, "Yea, yea."

Then the detectives began to ask about his cellphone (323) 804-7768 which was becoming his Achilles heel. He had to wonder why he ever got that cellphone. For months Maria Quijano had been constantly calling him begging him to kill her husband. Then on the night of the shooting he gave the hitmen his cellphone to use to call Maria. If only he didn't have that cellphone, he wouldn't be in this "fine kettle of fish." (Phrase made famous by Laurel and Hardy meaning being in a Fine Mess.) The detectives wanted to pin Oscar down as to being the sole user of that cellphone. Oscar said that he had used that cellphone for over three years and was the only person to use it.

Since the use of the phone was no longer an issue, the detectives moved on to discuss how well he knew Reynaldo and Maria Quijano. Oscar was more than willing to explain to the detectives he knew both of them. He went on to say that the reason he had contact with both of them was the fact that his son had rented a room from them. As a result, Oscar came regularly over to the Quijano home on Arcola Avenue basically to see his son.

On one occasion Reynaldo and Oscar worked on a car in the driveway. The best way to describe their relationship was cordial and friendly. He wanted to be pleasant with Maria since she seemed amiable enough to him. Over the years he felt sorry for Maria since her husband didn't spend much time with her. She was lonely and showed a suggestive interest in him.

Oscar went on to say that he had contact with Maria on April 9th. The detectives wanted to focus on how and why he called her on that date. Oscar explained that he owed Maria money for his son staying at their house. When pressed Oscar said he most likely talked to her four times between 9:00 p.m. and 10:30 p.m.

When the detectives asked Oscar what he was doing on the night of April 9th he quickly responded that he was home with some old friends. Then the interrogation took an inexplicable turn. As the detectives zoomed in on the use of his cellphone on the night of April 9th, Oscar claimed that someone robbed him and took his cellphone. What seemed curious was the fact that nothing else was taken from Oscar except his cellphone.

To embellish his story, he claimed it was taken at gunpoint. Then he added a kicker when he said that the robber of his cellphone was Wilson Sanchez. The one detective leaned back in his chair and had a skeptical look on his face. He said, "Let me get this straight. The other arrestee with you, Wilson Sanchez, was the person who robbed you of your cellphone." Oscar put his head down staring at the table in front of him. Oscar almost inaudibly uttered the words, "Yea yea."

The detective wasn't going to let Oscar sweep this under the carpet. He fired off the next question as to when Wilson Sanchez robbed him of his cellphone. Oscar tried to do some fast thinking by saying 11:00 p.m. Then maybe it was 9:00 p.m. As he was trying to peg the time, he voluntarily said that he saw another male inside Wilson's brown van. When pressed as to a description of that person he was vague and claimed he didn't get a good look at him.

The detective didn't know how long Oscar was going to try to sell this unbelievable story. Then the detective asked Oscar if he reported to the police this robbery of his cellphone by Wilson Sanchez. Oscar's creative thinking took another turn. He replied he didn't need to since about 45 minutes later Wilson returned and gave him back his cellphone. At that point the detective had to wonder if he had accidentally walked into the 'biggest liar's contest.'

The detective didn't know how to react. He realized that Oscar was trying his hardest to place his cellphone into someone else's possession. Since he had given it to Wilson then it seemed natural to claim Wilson had it. However, Oscar hadn't thought how to explain the fact that Wilson knew where the Quijano's house was located in Sun Valley. When asked, Oscar vehemently denied telling Wilson the directions to victim's home.

Oscar had tried his best to explain why he didn't have his cellphone around the time of the shooting. But he cooked his goose when he admitted that Wilson returned the phone to him 45 minutes. At that point he was admitting that he possessed the cellphone during the time that numerous phone calls were made by Maria to his cellphone.

The detective's look of disbelief made Oscar exclaim in a loud voice that he was telling the truth. The interrogation wasn't resulting in Oscar coming clean. The detectives had the phone records that proved Oscar wasn't being truthful. The detectives finished off by saying that when he was willing to tell the truth they would be willing to listen. They stood up to leave. Oscar had a befuddled look on his face.

The next day the detectives were busy doing reports. They wondered if Oscar had changed his mind about telling the truth. So, they had Oscar brought out so they could clarify some of the things he tried to sell them the night before. As Oscar came into the small interrogation room, he started off by claiming that he was sorry about what he had said last night.

The detective realized that this might be the moment they had waited for when someone would open up and tell the truth of what actually happened. Oscar seemed to want to get something off his chest but he didn't want to look like he was the bad guy in this situation. "Alright, Maria kept after me to find someone to kill her husband." Oscar couldn't look the detectives in the eye. He raised up both arms in a wave of frustration. "What could I do? She kept pestering me. It wasn't my idea." Then with a moment of silence he shook his head in disbelief. "For several months she kept asking. After a while it was easier to tell her that I would look for someone to do the killing." Oscar was hoping to get a sign of understanding from the detectives. However, the detectives were busily writing notes.

Oscar wanted to be recognized as a human being in a difficult situation. "Eventually I told her that I wouldn't do the killing but I would find someone else who would." This seemed to satisfy her at first. "I didn't know anyone who would do a killing. Where do you look for a hitman? I didn't know where to start. Every time I talked to her, she kept telling me plans how to do the killing. I tried to explain to her all the details that had to be worked out like the location."

He related that, "She didn't want Death in her home. Her idea was that he should be killed at work or possibly over at his girlfriend's place. Ultimately, she wanted answers as to how much it was going to cost her. At first I kept telling her that the price of a hit all depended on the circumstances."

The detectives were learning more than their cheap ballpoint pens could write. One of the detectives had gotten his pen from a real estate agent he had interviewed on another case. The other detective had picked up his 'el cheapo' pen from an insurance company. He continued to shake the pen to get the ink to come out in order to continue to write. After listening to Oscar for 13 minutes this detective gave up on his cheap ballpoint pen and decided to rely on the tape recorder which was taking down every word.

That detective who decided not to be the scribe just sat back to listen to dejected Oscar. As he listened to Oscar, he couldn't help but wonder how hitmen set their fees for killing someone. As a homicide detective, he had heard that killers will knock someone off for as little as a $100. Even others are willing to kill another human being for a mere fix of narcotics. There doesn't seem to be a fixed rate schedule that all hitmen agree on.

Other professions don't have fixed rates for performing services. Like a plumber or even a dentist there isn't a sliding scale for services. Some will charge as much as they can. However, most professionals are looking for repeat business so they don't charge exorbitated fees. Hitmen on the other hand don't rely on repeat business unless they are in some type of organized crime.

The detective felt like this was the perfect time to ask about hit fees. Oscar wanted to appear to be cooperative so he was willing to be honest as to how much a hit cost. He admitted that he was no expert on the going rate for a hit in Los Angeles in this day and age. When Maria was pestering him about what it would cost, he finally went to a local gas station to find out the going rate for a hit.

Oscar found a 'grease monkey' working on an oil change. He came up to the side of him and in a whispered voice asked him if he knew any bad dudes who would take care of someone who was bothering him. Without missing a beat, the greasy character said, "It all depends." Oscar was delighted that the guy was willing to discuss such a delicate issue with him. Oscar followed the garage mechanic as he started to check the transmission fluid.

Oscar in a hushed voice said, "It's a wife wanting to get rid of her husband." The grease monkey indicated that type of hit could run from

$8,000 to $20,000 depending on the location and who the victim was. Oscar complained to the guy that was a lot of money. By then the guy was working at the rear end of the car looking for oil leaks. His response was that you get what you pay for. If you want a clean job and to get away with it then it will cost something over $10,000.

By then the detective had heard more than he wanted to hear about the going rate for a hit. Then he directly asked how much did Oscar finally charge Maria. In a gesture to show how fair Oscar was as an individual he said that he told Maria that the killing of her husband would cost $8,000. Her reaction was that it was too much for a hit. After days of reflection over the amount, she told him that she was willing to pay $8,000.

Next, he explained that she needed to pay that money up front. This was the big sticking point since she claimed she didn't have large amounts of cash around. Her comment to Oscar was how could she trust the hitmen to do a clean job. At that point Oscar smiled at the detective and said, "I told her that if she wanted the job done, she needed to hand over the $8,000 in cash. Somehow, she was able to get that amount of money and handed it over to me."

CHAPTER 19 WHO HAS THE MONEY?

The detectives had the suspect talking, but was he willing to reveal who he gave the money to? The detective inquired, "What did you do with the money?" Oscar hesitated for a moment then looked up at the detective and gave him a sheepish look. "Well I didn't know what to do since I didn't know anyone who would kill another person. I felt trapped since I had received the money but I didn't know where to find someone to do the killing."

"Around April 9th, Maria started complaining that the killing needed to occur immediately since her husband was about to leave for El Salvador." Oscar was still sitting in the hot seat raising his arms up in frustration. "What was I supposed to do?" Then Oscar related the desperation that he felt. He checked around the neighborhood looking for anyone who appeared sleazy. Oscar explained that he was fearful to approach hardened gang members since he feared they would take the money from him.

Then on April 9th around 5:00 p.m. he saw several young taggers who he had often seen spend their evening loitering on the street corner. They didn't look very threatening but they most likely had no reservation about graffitiing someone's wall or garage door. Oscar didn't know how to go about soliciting them to do a Murder. He approached a group who seemed to be sharing a joint together. In a semi-joking way, he asked any of the guys if they knew anyone who could knock off someone.

These guys were older teenagers who didn't have steady jobs but just liked standing around doing nothing. Their main form of transportation was riding an old beat-up bike they had stolen from someone in another area. These guys listened to Oscar but didn't pay much attention since older people would try to get them to do something for nothing. It wasn't until Oscar explained that he was willing to pay someone $8,000 to knock someone off. Apparently, the sum of $8,000 did raise the curiosity of these graffiti artists. They inquired as to what had to be done and they showed a mild interest in the proposition.

When Oscar said that the killing had to take place in the San Fernando Valley, that was when he lost the interest of the taggers who only dreamed of having an automobile someday. Oscar claimed that Wilson Sanchez came by as he was talking and he started showing some interest. He inquired as to what exactly would he have to do for the $8,000. Oscar said all he had to do was shoot an old guy in Sun Valley. Wilson focused on what was of most interest to him, which was the money.

Wilson was only 20, but he was wise for his age. His response was, "Show me the money." Oscar tried to assure him that he had the money and it was all in cash. Wilson hadn't just fallen off the 'Turnip Truck.' Oscar didn't know what to do since his wife was home and he didn't feel comfortable taking some stranger into their apartment so he could show him the money. At that point, the taggers all started discussing what area they wanted to spray with graffiti that night. Oscar was pushed to the side since he wasn't relevant to the taggers' conversation.

Oscar had just received a call from Maria who sounded desperate in that it had to be done that night since her husband would be leaving town in the morning. With this dire plea from Maria, Oscar shoved his way back into the group of taggers. He nodded to Wilson and said, "Come with me." Wilson took the hint and followed Oscar into his apartment unit where he was shown the $8,000. The money was in hundred- and twenty-dollar bills.

Wilson and Oscar returned to the group standing on the street corner. Wilson told his buddies that he had never seen that much stash in cash. Then Wilson moved on to the next question which was who did they need to kill and where was it to take place. Oscar was prepared to answer those questions. He walked over to his green Honda to retrieve several items from the console between the front seats.

He returned to the group and handed Wilson a photo of a middle-aged Hispanic male. Oscar said, "That's the guy to kill." Then Oscar handed a map to Wilson which showed the location of the house where the killing was to occur. Wilson picked up the map and shook his head saying, "That's a long way to go." Oscar tried to reassure him that it wasn't that far. He said, "It's almost next to the Burbank Airport. It's not that far if you take the Harbor Freeway to the Golden State Freeway."

Wilson looked at his old Ford van parked next to the curb and said, "Well I guess it can make it." When Wilson started to inquire about having the use of a gun, Oscar shook his head and said, "You'll have to use your own." Since Wilson wanted to appear like a seasoned hitman, he didn't pursue the issue. He motioned to his closest buddies to follow him to his van. Oscar picked up his cellphone and called Maria and advised her that the hitmen were on their way.

At that point in the interrogation Oscar sat back in his chair thinking that he had told the detectives enough to get them off of his back. He had explained that he didn't do the shooting and named the person who left to do the job. In his mind he had told the truth and as a result, he should be released from custody.

But the detectives weren't finished with Oscar since they knew that there were many more phone calls he hadn't accounted for. Also, his statement only told half the story. Now the detectives asked the proverbial question "What happened next?" Oscar didn't really want to go on with his story but could see that he didn't have a choice.

Oscar related that Wilson came back to his apartment in about 40 minutes wearing gloves and had a dark hoodie on. He seemed to be out of breath and only said, "We did it." To be on the safe side he called Maria to get confirmation that Reynaldo was actually dead. When he was able to reach her on her cellphone, he expected to hear a joyous woman exclaim that she was so happy that her husband was dead. All he received from Maria was the question as to when were they going to do it?

Oscar was surprised and for her part Maria was flabbergasted as well. She told Oscar not to pay the so-called hitmen since her husband was alive and well in the bedroom. Oscar turned to Wilson and exclaimed that the victim was still alive. Oscar explained to the detectives that this became a tense moment for him. When he confronted Wilson with the fact that the victim was alive, Wilson pulled out a gun that he had acquired to do the hit. Wilson pointed the gun at Oscar and told him he wanted the $8,000 cash that he knew Oscar had in his house.

Oscar kept telling Wilson that he hadn't done the job. But Wilson said that they had driven out to the location and that the victim's Mercedes was already parked in front of the house. Wilson complained that he couldn't get to the victim since they never saw him in his car. That was when the wife got involved in the confrontation and said that she would definitely get her husband to go outside so the hit guys would have a chance to shoot him. Wilson argued how could he be certain that the victim would come outside.

Wilson said that he would go out there one more time but Oscar had to come along. Oscar didn't want to be involved in the actual shooting. He suggested that he would give Wilson his cellphone which he could use to call the wife when he was ready to have the husband sent outside to be shot. This seemed to be a reasonable solution as Oscar handed over to Wilson his cellphone. Wilson went along with this new arrangement.

Oscar could see Wilson walk back to his brown van and get in and take off. He could barely make out that another occupant was in the van. Oscar was glad that the nail-biting situation had been resolved and he wasn't being pestered by phone calls from Maria. It was a little more than an hour that Wilson returned to Oscar's apartment. This time he was on Oscar's cellphone talking to the wife. He handed the phone over to Oscar to talk to the wife.

She confirmed that her husband was dead and that Oscar could hand over the $8,000 to the hitman. Everyone was happy. Maria had a dead husband and she would get his life insurance. Wilson was ecstatic that he had earned more money than he had ever had in his life. Finally, Oscar had Maria off his back and could wash his hands of the entire mess.

The detectives listened intently and wondered why did he admit to being the middleman in this conspiracy to commit Murder. What was never clear was what did unlucky Oscar get out of this killing. Did he get the $20,000 that he had originally told Maria that a hit would cost and just pocketed the rest of the money?

Now the detectives had Maria, Oscar and Wilson in custody but none of the stories were consistent. It was as though the detectives had opened a can of worms in which the maggots were wiggling in all different directions. The detectives knew they had the bad dudes in jail but how were they ever going to prove Murder charges against all three of them?

What other persons were involved? The detectives had investigated the other calls made from Oscar's cellphone. What was surprising was that they came back to relatives or friends of both a Pablo Alvarenga and Erik Monroy. The surveillance detectives saw both Pablo and Erik in the brown van when they were following Wilson. The detectives knew that both young men were involved in some way, but they needed to interview both of them to hear their side of the story. The $64,000 Question was what was their connection to the Murder.

CHAPTER 20-PABLO OPENS UP

Pablo Alvarenga came across the detectives' radar in two totally different ways. The first was when the surveillance team saw Pablo traveling in the old brown van with Wilson. The other mention of his name came from Wilson himself who claimed that Pablo was his getaway driver. When the arrests and searches occurred, Pablo was nowhere around. It wasn't until May, 19, 2005, they were able to track him down and arrest him.

When they sat down for an interview of Pablo, they advised him of his Miranda Rights which he willingly waived. The detectives had run his criminal history and learned that he had prior run-ins with the law. As a juvenile he had a robbery and vandalism.

The detective didn't know exactly how this 18-year-old fit into this homicide but they wanted to hear from him. So, the detectives started asking a few nonconfrontational questions in hopes he would divulge something they didn't know. For all the polite talk, Pablo was like a clam not willing to open up and reveal any pearls of wisdom. The most that Pablo was willing to say was that he had known Wilson for years and the two had hung out together. He assured the detectives that he didn't know anything about a homicide that his pal Wilson was involved in.

The detective realized that this initial interrogation of Pablo was a big nothing and it was concluded. Later they realized that his phone number of 759-3250 was linked to a call that was made from Alvarado's cellphone the night of the Murder. As the detectives meticulously went down each call made from Alvarado's cellphone on the night of the shooting, they came across a phone number 795-3250 which was listed to a Martha Gomez (pseudonym).

Eventually the detectives starting asking harder questions. The one detective accused Pablo of lying to him. Pablo recoiled back in his chair as though he was shocked being called a liar. He tried to clear his throat and audibly said, "What do you mean?" Then the detective showed Pablo the phone records of Alvarado's phone. He pointed to the number 795-3250 on the phone record and said, "Look, that phone number was called at 11:46p.m., 12:25a.m. and 12:43a.m. Isn't that your mom's phone number?"

Pablo's eyes were hooked on the phone record. He sat frozen in his seat. His mind went into overdrive as to what should he say. The last thing in the world was that he didn't want to get his mom in trouble with the law. He felt compelled to say something. But the question was how much should he say and what should he say?

"Okay I was with Wilson Sanchez in the van on the night of the shooting. I guess I made those phone calls from Mr. Alvarado's phone." Then he went on to spin another scenario in which he wasn't involved in the shooting. He volunteered that he and his friends were hanging around 84th Street when an old guy came up to talk about "doing some shit." The old guy gave some money to Wilson and they went to some place in the San Fernando Valley. There the old guy got out and did the shooting and ran back to the van.

The detective gave Pablo a skeptical look, like don't try to pull the wool over my eyes. Pablo jerked back in his chair wondering what he had said wrong. The detective told Pablo that wasn't true since the old guy hardly could walk. Pablo thought for a minute and mulled it over as to what he had said. His mind continued to churn trying to think of what to say. He didn't want to admit to any involvement by himself. But he realized that his only hope was to implicate his old buddy Wilson Sanchez.

As though he wanted to appear to be coming clean, he said, "It was Wilson who did the shooting; however, it was the old guy who drove the van. He went on to say that the old guy supplied the gun that was used in the shooting. At all times Pablo tried to make it appear that he was as pure as the white driven snow. But as the story seemed to unravel, he admitted to going with these guys to the shooting. He wanted the detective to know that he didn't accept any money from the hit. The most he would admit to was that his buddy Wilson received all the money from Alvarado.

At no point did Pablo mention or name Erik Monroy as being present or having any involvement in the shooting. He seemed willing to burn his close friend Wilson but for some reason he wanted to remain loyal to his other longtime crony Erik. That was the most that Pablo would admit at least up until December 12, 2006, when it was time to make a pact with the devil.

CHAPTER 21- IT'S ERIK MONROY'S TURN TO SING

The detectives tried to make sense out of the confusing facts that had been extracted from the various known suspects. Erik Monroy came late on the scene. He first came to the attention of the detectives when he drove up to where Wilson was living when they were executing the search warrants. Since Wilson was in Monroy's car, the detectives likewise spoke to Monroy but didn't detain him since up to that point no one had mentioned Erik Monroy as being involved with the shooting.

Initially when the detectives were checking out all the phone numbers called from Oscar's cellphone, they came across several area code (323) numbers. On contacting those parties who were called, the detectives didn't realize that they were Erik's mother and girlfriend. It wasn't until much later that those numbers were connected up to Erik.

Eventually the detectives got the picture that Erik was somehow implicated but HOW? Then on November 28, 2005, the detectives had a chance to personally talk to Erik. He had seen his two comrades, Wilson Sanchez and Pablo Alvarenga, taken into custody and charged with Murder. The detectives didn't know exactly how to start the interview since they didn't have much of anything on Erik.

To their surprise Erik admitted to having a small part in the shooting. He indicated that on April 9th Wilson had asked him to drive Wilson's old brown van. The reason being that Erik was the only one who had a valid driver's license. He claimed that he thought they were going to a party. They directed him to drive on the 110 Freeway and head northbound. He remembered that Wilson was talking on a cellphone to some lady, but he didn't pay any attention.

Then Wilson shouted out directions as to where to turn off and what streets to take. Erik said he was unfamiliar with the area so he concentrated on where he was told to go. All of a sudden Wilson hollered at him to pull over. After he stopped the van, Wilson jumped out and ran into the shadows. He lost sight of Wilson until he heard two gunshots and immediately thereafter Wilson came running back to the van and jumped back in. Erik indicated he immediately floored the van and drove away. Erik claimed he didn't know in advance what was going to happen. He feigned complete surprise to the shooting. The detectives didn't know what to believe but they didn't have any other evidence to dispute his story.

Months later the detectives sat down with him to clear up some loose ends they had regarding the shooting. At that time Erik began to supply a more complete scenario as to what really happened. This time he indicated that night, he had ridden his bike to 84th Street to meet up with his friends. He noticed an old man he later identified as Alvarado talking to his pal, Pablo. Soon after he talked to Pablo who claimed the old guy wanted someone to kill some dude that night. Pablo laughed it off however their buddy Wilson showed more interest in what the man was saying.

Wilson said he would do the job but first he wanted to see the money. The old guy showed Wilson the money so it was 'game on.' Erik explained that if he got some of the money, he would do the driving. Their other companion Pablo was brought in to be the lookout for cops while it was agreed that Wilson would be the one to take care of business.

As the detective asked for more details Erik seemed totally willing to tell all. He mentioned that they had to make two trips to the Valley since the first trip didn't work out. He claimed that they had no way to contact the lady to get her husband to come outside. Erik related that the second trip included taking along the old man's cellphone. He said they started to drive back out to the house in the Valley.

They realized that they were low on gas so they stopped at a local 76 gas station. The guys weren't exactly well-financed hitmen who had full wallets to spend on their hit job. It was Wilson's van and he was the one who would be $8,000 richer after the killing. The old van's gas gauge was lower than the "E" for empty. The question was how much gas to purchase without going bankrupt. Wilson knew that filling up the gas tank would cost over $50 so that was out of the question. He figured that he needed to invest $15 of his hard-earned money for a little more than a quarter of a tank of gas.

Since money was on Wilson's mind, he was smart enough to grasp that his two accomplices wanted to be compensated for their efforts. Wilson turned to Pablo and him and said that he would give them $500 for their help. At the time this seemed fair to both of them, so they all piled back into the timeworn van and headed for the Valley. When they got there, Wilson got out and used the phone to call the lady to get her to have her husband come out. Shortly thereafter, a middle-aged man came out and got into his car. He started up the engine and began to pull away from the curb. Wilson ran toward the driver's side of the victim's car and started firing.

Immediately afterwards Wilson ran back to the van and they took off. They headed back to 84th Street and pulled in and parked in front of Alvarado's apartment. Wilson went in and came out with the $8,000. He kept his promise and counted out $500 for each of his mates.

After listening for months to Maria, Alvarado, Wilson and Pablo, the detectives came to the conclusion that Erik Monroy was the one who was willing to be the most forthright. For the detectives, it was refreshing to have someone provide an honest account as to how the shooting took place. What Erik had done was to totally implicate himself in the shooting. In other words, the detective didn't have any problem building a case against Erik for conspiracy to commit Murder. However, the detectives' main challenge was how were they going to build cases against all five suspects.

CHAPTER 22- TIME TO MAKE A DEAL

Now the detectives had five suspects in custody and they were all charged with the Murder of Reynaldo Quijano. The realization set in that the detectives had the most evidence against the two light-weights Erik and Pablo. The shooter, Wilson, painted a picture of himself as a person doing a public service trying to rid the community of sexual predator of young children.

As to Maria, she never admitted that she intended to kill her husband. The most she would admit to was that she wanted someone to beat up her philandering husband. True, she should have realized that beating him up might cause his death, but would a jury convict her of Murder?

But the old guy, Alvarado, maintained that he didn't kill anybody and didn't get any money from the shooting. The incriminating evidence revolving around the gas bill didn't connect him to the killing. Also, the only eyewitness saw a younger male running toward the van. There was nothing connecting the old guy to the van. The main piece of evidence against him was the fact that he had been given a cellphone that Maria had called numerous times. Unfortunately, the cellphone wasn't registered to Alvarado but to another individual.

The detectives were well aware that any statement made by one co-defendant couldn't be used against another co-defendant during their joint trial. This was a long-standing legal rule the Criminal Justice System had adopted. It was believed that it was unfair to have the prosecution use the statements of one defendant against a co-defendant. In this case the prosecution couldn't use Wilson Sanchez's statements he gave to the detectives in which he claimed that Alvarado was the person who hired him and paid him to do the killing.

The appellate court's reasoning was that a defendant like Alvarado wouldn't have the opportunity to cross-examine the defendant like Wilson who had made the incriminating statement about Alvarado's involvement. Why couldn't the one defendant call the other defendant to testify and then examine him under oath as what he had said? This is where the Fifth Amendment of the American Constitution comes into play. One defendant like Alvarado couldn't force another codefendant like Wilson Sanchez to testify against his will. The detectives recognized the legal dilemmas they were faced with.

It didn't take a legal beagle to recognize that if the prosecution wanted to build cases against all five parties to this conspiracy, the DA's Office would have to arrange some type of plea bargain in order to get one of the suspects to be willing to testify against the other suspects. In other words, one of the suspects would have to be given immunity or leniency.

Contract Killings are one of the most problematic cases for a prosecutor to deal with. By definition a Contract Killing occurs when one party hires another party (better known as the hitman) to kill an individual. It involves an illegal agreement between the parties in which one party agrees to kill a person in exchange for a payment.

Contract Killings can be confused with Assassinations. The main difference is that in an assassination the killer is motivated by some political or religious reason instead of gaining money.

Contract Killing aren't just challenging for prosecutors but also are more difficult to solve by law enforcement. The hiring party is more difficult to catch since he or she has no contact with the crime scene. Therefore, there won't be any eyewitnesses who could identify the hirer.

Also, there won't be any forensic evidence such as fingerprints or DNA left at the crime scene. And since the hirer isn't using the gun, there will be no ballistic evidence tying the hirer to the crime. As to the killer, law enforcement won't have motive evidence pointing to the killer since the hitman may never have had any contact with the victim.

There isn't any formula that can be used to show who is more sinister, the hirer or the hitman. Some people like to claim that both the hirer and the hitman are equally culpable. That is an oversimplification. Every Contract Killing situation has factors which may make the hirer or the hitman look more sympathetic or more sinister. When evaluating the parties' culpability, the prosecutor has to consider a number of factors.

As to the HIRER

What was the Relationship of hirer to the victim? Was it a domestic situation like we have in this case? Or was it a business relationship? Or could it be a situation in which the hirer sees the victim as an obstacle that needs to be removed in order for the hirer to accomplish a certain goal?

Another factor to consider is what was the hirer's Motive for killing the victim? Had the victim abused the hirer? Was the killing committed by the hirer to force the victim to stop the abuse? Or was the hirer more interested in gaining money? Or was the hirer more interested in getting rid of the victim so the hirer could have a new relationship with someone else?

Another factor slightly different from the Motive is the Malice the hirer has against the victim. This Malice can take the form of the type of killing the hirer requests. Does the hirer want the victim to suffer while being killed? If the hirer wants the victim to slowly die as can occur in a poisoning or strangulation this may be considered more malicious. If the killing is by a shot to the back of the head the death is instantaneous with little or no suffering.

Yet another consideration may be how long has the hirer planned to do this killing. If the killing is a spur-of-the-moment killing this may be a mitigating factor. However, when a hirer has spent months if not years planning and working out all the details, this may be considered an aggravating factor.

Along the same lines is the amount of money the hirer is willing to pay a hitman to do the killing. Should that be a factor in deciding culpability? The higher the amount one is willing to pay, the more it could be interpreted as greater Malice against the victim.

The detectives were aware of situations where the hirer paid only $500 to the hitman to do the killing and in another case $10,000 was paid. There doesn't seem to be a rate structure for hiring hitmen. Often it is how much the hirer can come up with in a limited amount of time.

CHAPTER 23- WHAT ABOUT THE REST?

As to the HITMAN

When considering the culpability of the hitman the issue of amount of money paid may be highly relevant just as discussed under the Hirer. Although the entertainment industry glamorizes hitmen, most people dislike so-called professional hitmen who charge large sums for their services. On the other hand, a down-on-his-luck hitman charging a modest amount may be considered less culpable. That type of person is doing the killing for money he needs just to exist.

Besides the amount for the hit, the one factor that makes the hitman appear to be more culpable is how many hits he has done. A true professional is one who looks upon the killing as merely a job. This type of person has no conscience and is willing to do another hit whenever the opportunity presents itself. This type of individual is labeled as a 'Cold Blooded Killer.' This type of killer doesn't consider whether the victim suffers, or that innocent parties might be accidentally hit.

As to the MIDDLEMAN

Not all Contract Killings have a middleman as in our present case. Often the hirer doesn't have the contacts or wherewithal to find and hire a hitman. The middleman is a person on the fringe. He isn't thought to be too culpable since he doesn't possess the intent to kill like the hirer or have the willingness to actually do the killing. In determining the culpability of the Middleman, one has to consider what if anything did, he get out of it.

If he helps out the hirer because he likes him or her then he is thought to be less culpable. On the other hand, if he is receiving money for procuring the hitman then he would be considered more culpable.

As to ACCOMPLICE

Certainly, the accomplice's culpability is directly related to what he or she exactly did. If the accomplice did something that facilitated the hitman to carry out the killing, then he is more culpable. However, if he or she merely provided information to the hitman in order to find the victim, then that may not be as serious. An accomplice may take many shapes and sizes. A person who merely supplies a vehicle to commit the killing isn't as culpable as the actual driver of the getaway car.

A person who supplied the Murder weapon would be more culpable if they knew the gun was to be used in a killing. A 'Look Out' may be less culpable if he or she is far removed from the actual killing. Very often the accomplice is a person who could never do the killing on their own but only gets involved in order to help someone out.

There are many factors to consider as to the accomplice involvement. The lesser the involvement the lesser the culpability.

Up to this point we have reviewed the various roles in Contract Killings. In our present case we have a

HIRER who was Maria Quijano

HITMAN who was Wilson Sanchez

MIDDLEMAN who was Oscar Alvarado

ACCOMPLICE who were Erik Monroy and Pablo Alvarenga

The DA's Office needs to determine who of this group is less culpable and make a plea bargain offer to obtain their cooperation and testimony against the others. As we have seen in the above discussion, there are many factors that need to be considered when deciding culpability. The best way to evaluate a co-conspirator's culpability is to look to other cases in which the DA's Office had to give either immunity or leniency to parties in a Contract Killing.

Your author has written several books about Contract Killings which are worth reviewing at this point to determine culpability in our present case.

The Mickey Thompson killing is a good example of the parties involved in the killing. The facts of the Thompson case involved a business partnership between two auto racing giants. Mickey Thompson, the more famous promoter, realized his partner Goodwin wasn't paying his fair share of the expenses. As a result, Mickey sued Goodwin and won the civil lawsuit. Goodwin refused to pay the judgment and Mickey started to attach Goodwin's' assets. This legal dispute went on for years and ultimately went up to the US Supreme Court which found in favor of Mickey Thompson.

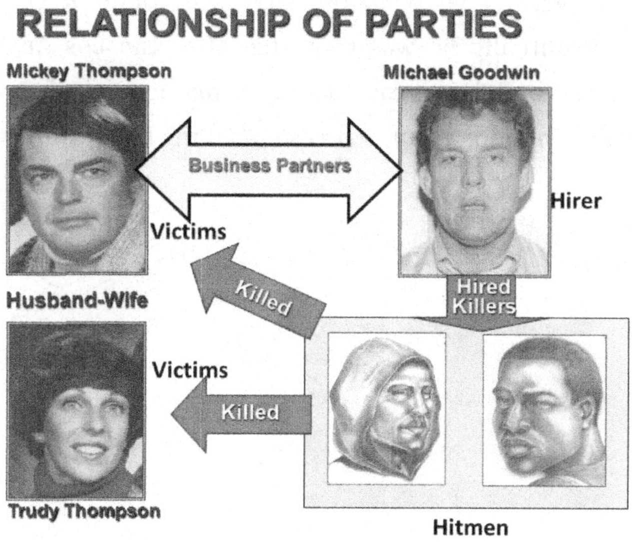

Goodwin couldn't accept the loss so he tried to find a way of getting back at Mickey. Goodwin knew that Mickey dearly loved his wife, Trudy, who helped him immeasurably operate their extensive auto racing business. His ex-partner felt that nothing would hurt Mickey more than having him watch his beloved wife being killed before his own eyes. Goodwin hired two black men to shoot Trudy on the driveway of their home. They made Mickey watch the killing of his wife and then shot Mickey in the head moments later.

This was the classic Contract Killing case where Goodwin the ex-partner was the hirer. It was never known for certain where Goodwin hired the two black men. It was believed that the hitmen may have been from Jamaica and after the shooting they most likely returned to their home country. In other words, this was such a difficult case to prosecute since the Jamaican hitmen were never apprehend. At the time many people believed Goodwin was the hirer but there weren't any eyewitnesses or any forensic evidence connecting him to the crime scene.

It took over 20 years before the case could be prosecuted against Goodwin. Eventually he was convicted after the Los Angeles DA's Office spent months building a case based on his actions of trying to cover his tracks. To learn more about that case, read my book ***Killing of a Legend.***

CHAPTER 24 OTHER TOUGH CONTRACT KILLINGS

Another Contract Killing case involved Rebecca Cleland who was the estranged wife of the victim. She wanted her husband killed so she could collect on his life insurance policies and gain all of his assets. The wife Rebecca was definitely the hirer. Initially she tried to get her sister to find a hitman since the sister worked at a bail bond business. When the sister refused, Rebecca looked elsewhere, but after several months she realized that she wasn't going to find any reliable hitmen.

That was when Rebecca turned to her cousins. Her one cousin Jose had a drug problem and was always in need for money. It didn't take cousin Jose long to come up with a gun. She got her other cousin Alvaro to be the accomplice and he drove the getaway vehicle. Then one evening she invited her estranged husband to get together with her for dinner at a Mexican restaurant in East Los Angeles.

After dinner, she did the driving and drove to a dark secluded area where she stopped the car to check something out. Cousin Jose came out of the bushes and started shooting at the husband who was seated in the car. The victim tried to escape and ran across the street where Jose shot him in the back of the head. Afterwards the shooter ran to the getaway car driven by cousin Alvaro.

In this case, Rebecca was the hirer, Jose was the hitman and cousin Alvaro was an accomplice. The issue was could all three be prosecuted together without having to give immunity or leniency to any one of them. Fortunately for the prosecution Rebecca had made some incriminating statements to friends which helped the prosecution. But what incriminated her more was that she continued to wear her wedding ring which she had claimed was stolen at the time of the shooting.

As to the cousin Jose who did the shooting, he got tripped up by using the borrowed gun. But what convicted the cousin who was the accomplice getaway driver was the cellphone evidence that showed that he was in the area of the shooting when it occurred. If you want to learn more about this Contract Killing read my book ***Honeymoon with a Killer***.

Lastly there was one other Contract Killing in which the DA's Office had great difficulty prosecuting all the parties involved. Factually it was similar to the Rebecca Cleland case in that it involved a wife, Claudia Haro, who wanted to kill her ex-husband. The ex-wife had difficulty finding a reasonable, responsible hitman. She hired one guy to shoot her ex but he claimed he got lost looking for where the ex was living. He insisted that he had earned the money and refused to give the money back to the wife, the so-called Hirer, even though he had not even attempted to shoot the victim.

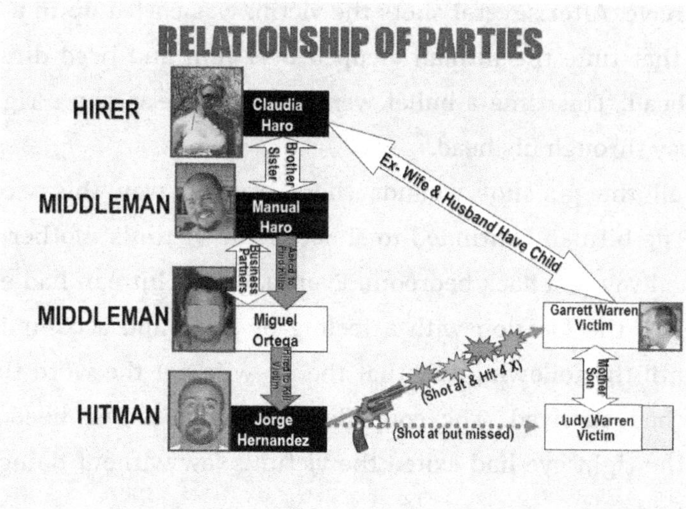

What made this case complicated was the fact that the ex-wife had to turn to her brother to find a hitman. The brother wasn't the type who was willing to go directly over to the ex-husband and shoot him. He was a big guy who had been involved in various scrapes with the law. The brother turned to a friend and asked him to find a hitman. In the end there were two MIDDLEMEN involved. Eventually the second MIDDLEMAN tracked down a person who was willing to do the hit for $10,000. But again, how reliable was this new hitman likely to be?

This hitman seemed to be responsible in that he was able to find the house where the ex-husband was living with his mother. He knocked on the front door and eventually the victim opened the door just a crack to see who it was. The hitman said that he had hit a car and he wondered whether the car in the driveway was the victim. Naturally the victim opened the door wider to see if his car was damaged or not.

Without another word being spoken the hitman pulled a handgun out of his waistband and fired it directly at the victim. The shot propelled the victim to fly backward. The hitman wanted to make sure that the victim didn't survive. After several shots the victim was curled up in a ball on the floor. At that time the hitman stepped over him and fired directly at the victim's head. This time a bullet went through the victim's right eye and tore its way through his head.

With all the gunshot wounds there was no way this victim would survive. The hitman continued to shoot at the victim's mother as she ran down a hallway to a back bedroom. Eventually the hitman had emptied his gun and left the location with a feeling of pride and accomplishment. It wasn't until the following day that the ex-wife got the word that her ex-husband had survived. The coup de grace shot to the head that went through the right eye had exited the victim's jaw without doing any harm to his brain.

The ex-wife was so furious and demanded her money back. The hitman felt bad that he hadn't accomplished the objective but still refused to return the thousands of dollars. He vehemently apologized and the best he would do was to promise that he would try again but she needed to pay him some more money. The ex-wife was so mad at everyone especially her brother who had promised that he had found a reliable hitman. For the price she was paying she thought there should be a guarantee. The hitman tried to explain that not everything works out the first time but next time he would definitely get the guy. The ex-wife was not so certain.

In this last example, who was most culpable? Obviously, the wife was the most culpable since she was so insistent that her ex-husband needed to be killed. Also, the hitman wasn't malicious but was only trying to do his job the best he could. However, the middlemen were the ex-wife's brother who liked the ex-husband but wanted to please his sister. Also, the brother's friend the other middleman wasn't getting anything out of this. He didn't have any skin in the game and was just trying to be helpful.

The DA's Office needed someone to cooperate to be able to prosecute the ex-wife and hitman. The prosecutors decided to use the second middleman to help make cases against all of the others. For more information about this unusual case you can read my book ***Killer at the Door***.

CHAPTER 25 - IMMUNITY AND LENIENCY

The previous chapter listed the factors that the prosecutor needs to consider when deciding to grant either leniency or immunity in order to convict the most culpable parties involved in the conspiracy to commit Murder. Prosecutors are aware that the public dislikes the idea of giving one criminal a break in order to get another criminal. However, sometimes the prosecutor has to do something that isn't popular in the mind of the public. All the prosecutor can do is evaluate the entire case and make a decision based on seeing that justice is done no matter how unpopular it may seem to some.

Often the elected district attorney has to bite the bullet and hope it isn't an election year. After the case is litigated the prosecutor can try to explain his or her decision to the public. However, it might be too late for the DA if the election occurs before the case is finally concluded.

An example of these type of tough decisions can be seen in what happened in the prosecution of Charles Manson. The Tate and La Bianca cases involved the brutal killing of seven victims. The case was solved when Susan Atkins told a cellmate that she and members of the Manson family did the killings. It was when the cellmate told LAPD detectives what Atkins had told her that the police compared all the family members' fingerprints to the latent prints found at both crime scenes.

It didn't take long before they found that a latent print on the front door of the Tate house matched Tex Watson's fingerprint. Also, Patricia Krenwinkel's print was lifted from a window shutter in the Tate house. Since Charles Manson didn't go to the Tate house to do the killings, his prints certainly wouldn't be found in the Tate house.

The prosecution had no forensic evidence against the ringleader Charles Manson. Susan Atkins' statement to her cellmate implicated Charlie as the person who planned and supervised the killings. However, the prosecutor couldn't use Atkins' statements against Charlie just like we can't use the co-conspirator's statements against the other co-conspirator.

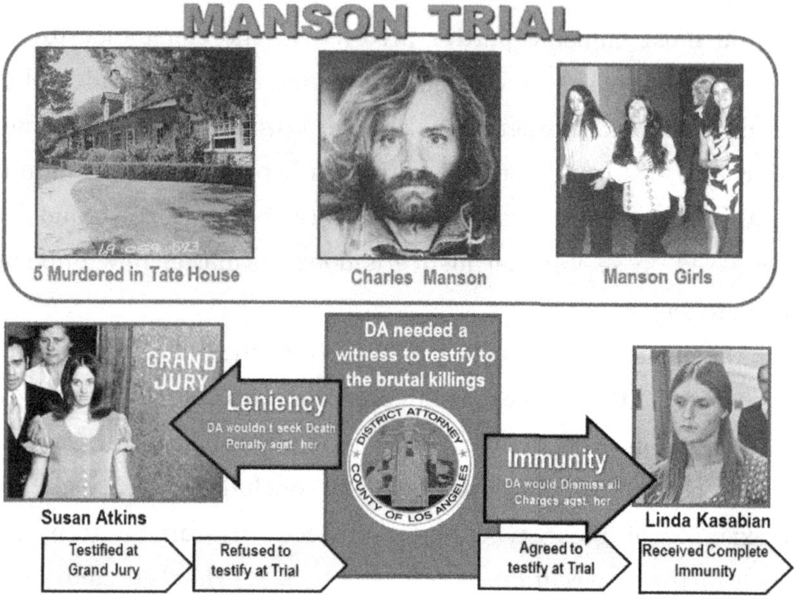

So, in the infamous Manson case, Charlie Manson, the mastermind of the killings, couldn't be prosecuted since there was no forensic evidence against him and any statements explaining his involvement couldn't be used. That was the time that the DA's Office was willing to grant leniency to Susan Atkins to get her to testify against her fellow family members who were involved in the killings. The DA agreed to forego the Death Penalty against her thereby permitting her to receive a Life sentence for her cooperation. Some members of the public were outraged that the DA was willing to give such leniency to Atkins, who admitted stabbing to death Sharon Tate and her fetus.

The DA's Office thought it was an appropriate plea bargain since they would have Susan Atkins testify against Charlie and the others. Her testimony would be enough to convict all the other members involved in the killings. Susan Atkins did testify before the Grand Jury and as a result of her testimony all the parties were indicted for Murder. However, not everything in life works out as planned. When it came time for trial, Susan Atkins refused to testify. All of a sudden it looked like Charlie Manson wouldn't be convicted and would be free to return to his so-called family.

Needless to say, panic set in when the prosecution saw this extremely brutal Murder of seven people blow up just before trial. There was consideration that maybe the DA needed to offer immunity to Susan Atkins to get her to change her mind. That would mean that the person who did the most brutal acts would go Scot Free.

Shortly before trial the attorney for Linda Kasabian floated the idea that maybe Kasabian would be willing to testify if she received complete immunity. At first the prosecution team didn't want to consider granting complete immunity to anyone. The most they would consider was working something out along the lines of leniency as to the sentence to be served. The clock was ticking away and the DA was becoming more desperate with every passing day. Then there was the discussion as to exactly what was Kasabian's involvement in the two separate killings.

As to the Tate killings, Kasabian was the lookout and she never went inside the Tate house. Likewise, she didn't go into the LaBianca house. The feeling was that she was the least culpable of all the family members.

As to the question as to how useful would she be as a witness, it appeared that she could testify to Charlie's involvement in the planning of the Tate killings. As to the LaBianca killings she could testify that she observed Charlie and Tex go up to the LaBianca house and come out and order the other girls to go up and do the killings with Tex Watson.

In the end the DA's Office gave Linda Kasabian complete immunity for her truthful testimony. After the trial she went on to enjoy a free and full life raising a family in a rural area of Maine. The Manson family members she testified against received a life sentence behind bars. Many members of the news media and public criticized the DA's Office for caving in and granting immunity to a criminal like Linda Kasabian.

Since leniency and immunity are such volatile issues, the LA DA's Office has a strict policy that must be followed when considering either of them. As to the present case, the DA's Office went through a lengthy process of evaluating which defendant should be considered for leniency or immunity.

As to Maria Quijano she was the HIRER in this Contract Killing situation. Generally, the hirer is not the type of person that the DA's Office wants to give leniency or immunity to. In reviewing the facts of the case, she initially claimed she knew nothing about her husband's death. She even went so far as to claim that she didn't hear the shooting or the noise from the responding vehicles. It wasn't until after she was arrested that she admitted that she had asked Oscar Alvarado to help her find someone to scare her husband by beating him up or damaging his car. She denied that she ever believed that the people Alvarado hired would go so far as to kill her husband.

Later she admitted that she obtained two prices from Oscar Alvarado. One was for killing her husband which was somewhere between $20,000 and $25,000. She indicated that was too much and she couldn't afford to have her husband killed. However, when Alvarado stated that she could have him beat up for under a $1,000, she figured that was the most that she could afford. As a result, she claimed that she paid Alvarado the money several months earlier for him to set up the assault.

Also, the prosecutors had to consider several other factors. There was always the possibility that a jury might feel some sympathy for Maria since her husband was a philanderer who was outright cheating on her. Also, there was the unsubstantiated issue that her daughter was raped by her husband. Although Maria's daughter didn't confirm such an allegation, it was one of those factors that could become the big elephant in the room. Even though she maintained that she didn't intend for her husband to be killed, her actions revealed an image of a wife who wanted to be rid of her husband so she could enjoy a new life paid for by his life insurance. When considering all the factors involved, she wasn't the type of co-conspirator who should be given leniency in order to obtain her testimony against the other co-conspirators.

As to Oscar Alvarado the so-called MIDDLEMAN, he might be the type that a DA would be willing to give a break to in order to convict the more culpable co-conspirators. He certainly didn't hatch the idea to kill Reynaldo. Also, he wasn't the type to play the role of the hitman. He gave the appearance of being a friend who was pressured into helping an acquaintance do a dastardly deed.

Yet, his hands might not be completely clean if in fact Maria paid him $20,000 for the hit and he gave only $8,000 to the hitmen and he pocketed the remaining $12,000. However, we will never know how much he received from Maria since he claims she gave him only a $1,000, when in fact we know that she gave at least $8,000 which the hitmen received.

Defendant Alvarado was a mixed bag. If he were used as a prosecution witness, his testimony would totally convict both Maria and Wilson. Without a doubt, he knew so much firsthand information about actions and statements of those two co-conspirators. However, where Alvarado could not be helpful to the prosecution was as to the accomplices Erik Monroy and Pablo Alvarenga. As a matter of fact, Alvarado didn't have any real contact with those accomplices. He couldn't testify to what they did with Wilson and the trips to Sun Valley.

Moving on to **Wilson Sanchez**, he was the hitman—the person who pulled the trigger. He wouldn't be a likely candidate to be given leniency or immunity. Yet, the DA's Office knew they would need some help from one of the suspects in order for everyone to be held accountable. Initially Wilson completely denied having any knowledge or information about the homicide.

Later he tried to justify his action on the fact that he thought the victim was a pedophile and that the victim deserved to die. At one point he claimed that he was having financial problems and he did the killing since he was desperate for money. This may be a mitigating factor but because he had not been truthful to the detectives the prosecutors didn't believe that he would be a credible witness.

Now the DA's Office was down to the two accomplices. Could either of them be relied on to tell the truth as to what happened? As to **Pablo Alvarenga** the prosecutors had to determine how involved he was in the actual shooting. The main problem with accomplices is that they may not have seen or heard enough to make them a useful witness for the prosecution. When the prosecution reviewed what Pablo had told the detectives the prosecutors learned that he was not completely candid at first.

He told the detectives that he knew Wilson Sanchez but knew nothing about a homicide. In a subsequent interview he explained that he saw Oscar Alvarado give money to Wilson and saw them leave in Wilson's van. He claimed that he didn't go with them but he seemed to indicate that Wilson probably was the shooter. The detectives were becoming more suspicious of Pablo constantly changing his story to fit the facts which had been uncovered.

The prosecutors recognized that Pablo was the least culpable of any of the co-conspirators. Also, he had been present at the time of the shooting and had seen Alvarado's involvement in hiring a hitman. However, it was hard for the prosecution to judge how credible he would be as a witness since he hadn't been truthful with the detectives.

Now the prosecution was at the bottom of the barrel when it came to **Erik Monroy**. The detectives hadn't considered him a suspect even though he had driven up to Wilson's place when the search warrants were conducted. In his initial interview with the detectives he only admitted knowing Wilson and had seen him on the night of April 9th. As to the shooting, he claimed he knew nothing about it. However, over time his name came up as one of the parties involved in using Alvarado's cellphone.

It wasn't until six months into the investigation that the detectives sat down and had an interview with him. He admitted that on the night of the shooting he had met with his friends Wilson and Pablo and was asked to drive Wilson's van to what he thought was a party. The reason they wanted him to drive was that he was the only one who had a valid driver's license. When the prosecutors reviewed Erik's statements to the detectives it became clear that he was being the most truthful of all of the co-defendants. They could see that since he was the driver, he could testify to Alvarado's involvement of hiring the guys to do the hit. Also, he could testify to Wilson's role in the shooting. Furthermore, he could explain Pablo's limited role as the 'look-out' and the obtainer of the gun. However, Erik couldn't testify to much about Maria's role in hiring someone to kill her husband. He had talked to a woman on the cellphone who wanted to know if he was the one who was going to do the job. Since he had never talked to Maria before he would have difficulty in identifying her voice as the hirer to this Contract Killing.

Now the prosecutors had to weigh a number of factors.

First, which of the suspects would be willing to take a plea bargain?

Second, what leniency or immunity would have to be given to that suspect to testify?

Third, how relevant would that suspect's testimony be in supplying crucial evidence against the others?

Fourth, how credible would this suspect be, especially if this person has told numerous lies previously?

After lengthy discussions and numerous memorandums being written, the DA's Office agreed that they would be willing to consider Leniency for both Erik Monroy and Pablo Alvarenga. But first the DA's Office wanted to obtain a proffered statement from them. The prosecutors wanted a complete truthful statement. These statements couldn't be used against them if the plea bargain didn't work out and they eventually went to trial. Once the proffered statements were obtained from both Erik and Pablo, then the prosecutors had the laborious task of trying to find sufficient corroborating evidence to support their testimony.

CHAPTER 26 - CORROBORATION

When a prosecutor decides to use an accomplice (co-defendant) to testify to the guilt of a defendant, the prosecutor needs to provide corroboration to support the accomplice's testimony. In this case the prosecution wanted to use both Pablo Alvarenga and Erik Monroy to testify to the planning of the crime, the shooting of the victim, and the payoff for the shooting. What that meant was that the prosecution needed to find other witnesses who could verify those accomplices' statements (testimony).

Tony Touch Aguilar (pseudonym) indicated that on the evening of April 9th, 2005, he remembered arriving at 84th Street and saw his buddies Pablo and later Wilson talking to an old guy who was trying to find someone who was willing to do a Murder for him. Shortly thereafter Erik arrived and joined his friends. Tony saw them all talking and noticed that the old guy walked across the street to a car to get a photo of the person to be killed. Further he recalled that there was talk about getting a strap (gun) in order to do the job. Then Tony Touch noticed that all of them left in Wilson's van to do the job.

Tony Touch definitely would be able to supply valuable corroboration since he personally can verify how both Pablo and Erik were in contact with Alvarado and Wilson on the night of the shooting.

Willis Barnes (pseudonym) would testify that he was a good friend of Wilson Sanchez as well as Erik Monroy. Late on April 9th and early on April

10, 2005, all three, Wilson, Erik and Pablo arrived at his house in Wilson's van. Wilson asked him if he would keep some money for safekeeping, Wilson had in an envelope. Barnes believed that the cash was in large bills and totaled around $9,000. After storing the cash in a safe place in his house, he joined the group in celebrating their good fortune.

Barnes remembered that his buddies told him that they shot some dude because he was molesting a woman's younger children. This woman wanted the victim dead for all the abuse he had caused her family. All of those facts further corroborated what Pablo and Erik claimed took place after the shooting.

Dorthey Perez (pseudonym) daughter of Maria could supply some corroboration in that she saw the victim's Mercedes parked in front of the house around 10:30 p.m. The two accomplices indicated that on the first trip to the house after 10:30 p.m. that the car was parked in front. Also, she indicated that she heard gunshots around midnight. This is the time that the accomplices said that they returned and did the shooting.

Serena Chavez (pseudonym) Erik's mother could testify that she received three calls from her son, on April, 9, 2005 at 11:25 p.m. , 11:28 p.m. , and 11:45 p.m. This verifies what Erik had told the detectives.

Karen Rosales (pseudonym) Erik's girlfriend could testify that she received one call from Erik on April 9, 2005 at 11:45 p.m. again this corroborates exactly what Erik had said to the detectives.

Martha Gomez (pseudonym) Pablo's mother could testify that she received three phone calls on April 9. 2005 at 11:46 p.m. 12:25 p.m., and 12:43 p.m. from her son. The same was true that his mother verified that Pablo had used Alvarado's cellphone to call his mother.

Sally Talles was a crucial witness in all of the defendants' trials. She was able to corroborate the fact that the van used had a window with paper over it. That was the way that the accomplices identified the vehicle they used.

Besides the above witnesses the cellphone records verified that Alvarado's cellphone was used by both accomplices at the time they had indicated. Along the same line, the cellphone towers were able to verify the exact time the accomplices had told the detectives that they were traveling the freeways to and from the Sun Valley location.

But one of the strongest pieces of corroboration was from the two accomplices. The fact that they both at the time of the proffered statements told consistent stories supplied a vital form of corroboration. Although Pablo had told numerous stories earlier to the detectives, both accomplices' proffered statements were almost 100% consistent. After reviewing all the evidence, the prosecutors believed that they had sufficient corroborating evidence to use either or both Pablo and Erik as prosecution witnesses.

CHAPTER 27- BUILDING A CASE

It didn't take long for the District Attorney's Office to recognize that this homicide case involving the killing of Reynaldo Quijano was exceedingly complex with so many defendants. Since the shooting occurred in Sun Valley, the case was assigned to the Van Nuys DA's Office in the Van Nuys courthouse. However, the local prosecutors didn't have the time to shepherd a five-defendant case, especially because of the heavy court calendars in the Van Nuys courthouse.

The District Attorney's administration contacted the DA's Major Crimes Division and instructed them to take over the Quijano case. Since Beth Silverman was considered the so-called "Valley Girl" for the DA's Office, it seemed only fitting to assign the Quijano case to her. For Beth Silverman, the Valley was her home and where she had grown up. She had tried so many of the Valley's homicide cases. She had gained a reputation of being the 'Terminator for Bad Dudes in the Valley.' She was so well known in the Valley she was on a first name basis with the Homicide detectives.

So, when Beth was notified that she was assigned the Quijano case, she didn't complain or say why dump that on me. All she said to her law clerk was, "Just place the Quijano file on top of my stack of pending Murder cases." Initially, Beth wasn't aware how big a migraine headache this case could be.

Later in the week when she didn't have any courtroom appearances, Beth pulled the Quijano case out of the tall stack of pending cases. It didn't take her long to locate the relevant police reports. She leaned back in her creaky county-issued chair. As was Beth's practice, she gripped the police report with both hands and her eyes scanned the contents for certain key words. While reading to herself she would inadvertently shake her head and mutter quietly the words, "Okay, we can handle that."

Beth doesn't waste her time on the irrelevant. She had read so many homicide reports that she knew exactly what to look for. After digesting the police reports her left hand automatically picked up the telephone while her right hand punched in the phone number for the LAPD North Hollywood Detective Bureau. Within minutes she was firing off questions to the detectives.

Beth didn't mess around with 'small talk' but directly asked why certain tests hadn't been done and why certain logical witnesses hadn't been interviewed. The detectives were used to conducting their own interrogations, but when Beth started questioning the detectives, they had to feel that the tables were turned and they were the ones being interrogated.

It isn't that Beth can't be socially charming, but when she is assigned a case it is time for her to focus on what needs to be done. Building a successful homicide case takes time and plenty of critical thinking. Beth is like a master chess player. She is thinking and planning five moves ahead. Experience has taught her that when it is time for the actual trial it is too late to research witnesses' backgrounds or to request forensic tests.

Months before trial, Beth is like a human dynamo barking out orders like a master drill sergeant. She knows the 'drill' and is only too aware of the unpredictable roadblocks. The bureaucracy in the police and coroner's Office as well as the DA's Office like to deny requests on the basis, "If you had given it to us earlier, we could have done it, but it is too late now." This isn't Beth's 'first rodeo' and she knows how to beat the Naysayers.

Since there were five defendants in this one case, the superior court judges could see this one case could tie up one courtroom for six months or longer. Such a lengthy trial can ruin an individual courtrooms' calendar for an entire year. As a result, the Quijano case was set in the downtown Criminal Court Building where there are numerous 'long cause' courtrooms which could accommodate such a lengthy trial.

As a result, the case was continued to find an available downtown courtroom. What that did was to give Beth sufficient time to get all of her ducks in a row. In 2006 Beth had contacted your author who had an office next door to her office. One day she came into my DA's office and said, "Ron, I need to find a way to explain this five-defendant case to the jury." I had worked with Beth on many convoluted cases even before she had been assigned to Major Crimes Division. We had spent hours creating PowerPoint slide presentations that she had used in other Opening Statements and Arguments.

Beth had earned a reputation as being a highly successful prosecutor. She was willing to try the most difficult cases and didn't avoid cases just because they were full of witness problems or legal issues. One of Beth's strong points is that she is capable of viewing a case the way jurors would see it.

Beth's other forte is that she knows precisely what needs to be done. Whenever I asked for certain items such as photo or document, she had it ready to hand over to me. When she didn't have something, she would make a note and within hours, her law clerk would bring it to me. As a result, it was a delight to work with such a persistent professional. However, there was a downside to working with Beth. That was she could be capricious when reviewing any presentation that had been prepared for her.

In her mind she visualized how something should appear and if it differed, she made it clear that it wasn't right. This often led to heated discussions in which egos could be bruised. I had learned early on that all presentations weren't chiseled in stone. All presentations have to be considered 'Drafts' that can be changed even up to minutes before being used in the courtroom. I knew that the world of the courtroom is highly dynamic. Last-minute changes can be caused by a judge making a last-minute ruling on the evidence or a witness failing to appear.

Tensions can run high when attorneys are in trial. Beth is no exception but when things are sorted out well in advance it reduces the eleventh-hour friction. I have found that Beth often will want last-minute changes and I merely ask her to mark up the draft the way she wants it done. 'Thank God for computers.' I will call up her file and within minutes the changes are made. As a result, Beth has her modified slide show or visual aids the way she wants it. Then she is ready to take on the many battles in the courtroom.

CHAPTER 28- OPENING STATEMENT

When it was decided to try Maria Quijano separately, I prepared a PowerPoint presentation which was tailored to the evidence that would be presented in her trial. The purpose of the Opening Statement is to provide the jurors a road map as to what evidence they will be hearing and seeing during the lengthy trial. Attorneys know that they will not be able to have their witnesses testify in a chronological or even in a logical order. Therefore, the Opening Statement is a way of explaining all the evidence to the jury in an understandable fashion. The idea is that when a witness has to be called out of order to testify, the jurors will be able to understand where that witness's testimony fits into the case.

On the day of the Opening Statement Beth was dressed in a dark professional woman's suit with a white strip around the collar and along the sleeves. She projected a subdued image of the attire worn by the female attorneys depicted on the old LA Law TV program. Her jet-black hair had been neatly combed and occasionally she would use her hand to pull it behind her ears. Beth would not be classified as a vain woman but she was well aware of the importance of projecting the proper aura in the formal courtroom.

As she stood up and walked over to the lectern, she wanted to command everyone's attention. She waited until there was complete silence before commencing her Opening Statement. She was acutely aware that an effective attorney doesn't waste precious face time in front of a jury with 'small talk.' Straight out of the box she went directly to the heart of her case.

She used a PowerPoint slide show to help her communicate the facts of the case to the jury. She had set up the projector in what is called the 'courtroom well,' which is the space between the judge's bench and the row of counsel tables. The projector showed her slides on a gigantic screen attached to the side wall of the courtroom. In this way all the jurors could clearly see what she was talking about.

Beth used her remote-control clicker to project her title slide which appeared on the screen behind her. Her next click of the remote caused the stark photo of the victim shot dead in his car in the middle of the street. In this way Beth wanted to impress the jurors that they were going to be required to make a thought-provoking decision whether this defendant was guilty of a cold-blooded Murder.

Beth started out by saying that on the night of April 10, 2005 at 12:15 a.m. a 39-year-old human being by the name of Reynaldo Misael Quijano was seated in his car in front of his house in Sun Valley where he was shot and murdered.

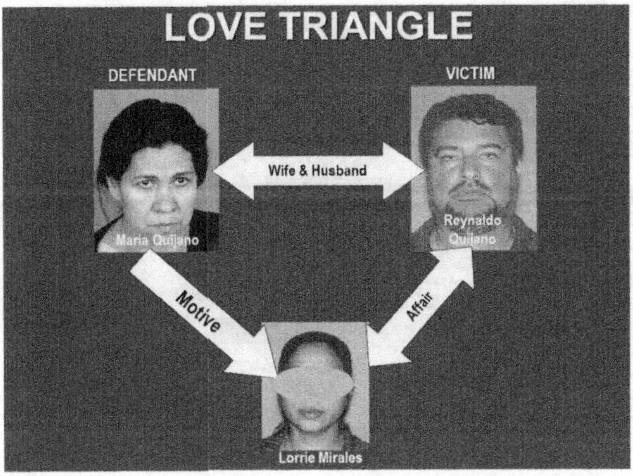

Next Beth flipped on the screen a slide showing the triangle relationship of the parties. It depicted photos of the defendant, Maria, with her husband. The prosecutor explained that the victim's wife, Maria Quijano, had her husband murdered. The slide was titled LOVE TRIANGLE showing the husband's girlfriend on the bottom. Beth used an arrow from the wife pointing toward the girlfriend with the word MOTIVE. She explained that was one of the reasons for the shooting. In this way the jurors quickly got the picture of the relationship of all the parties. (Many of the following slides have been slightly modified to obscure photos of parties and names changed in order to protect the innocent.)

Beth wanted to convey to the jurors that the killing was not entirely due to jealousy but also greed. That was when she spelled out the fact that the wife wanted to collect her husband's life insurance. The wife was listed as the beneficiary and would receive $225,000 upon her husband's death.

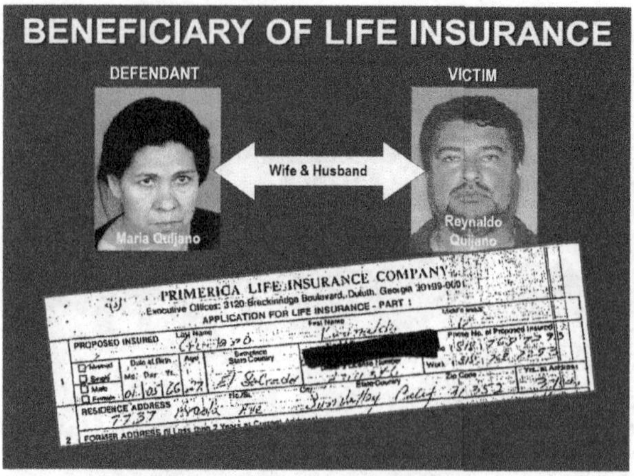

Beth couldn't afford having the jurors becoming lost in a web of characters involved in this Murder case. Her next slide was to show who was the 'Middleman' in the conspiracy to kill the husband. This slide showed that the defendant-wife had asked Rene Oscar Alvarado to find someone to kill her husband, Reynaldo.

Immediately, Beth wanted the jury to see that the defendant was seriously attempting to find someone to kill her husband. She discussed with the middleman, Oscar Alvarado, how the killing would take place, when, where as well as the cost of such a hit. Eventually the defendant paid Alvarado an amount somewhere between $8,000 to $26,000 to have her husband killed.

On her next slide, the prosecutor showed the bank records which proved that the defendant withdrew a large sum of money from her bank account.

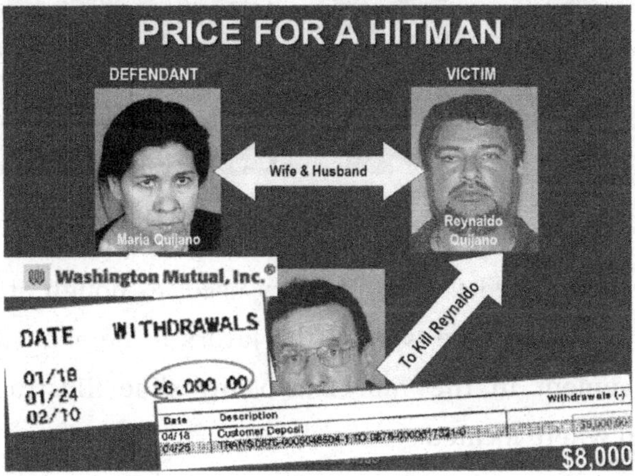

After she had discussed the Motive for the Murder, Beth wanted the jurors to be introduced to the entire cast of characters. She used the below slide to show the individuals who Alvarado had hired to kill the defendant's husband. At this point Beth introduced the hitmen to the jury and spelled out their role in the shooting. She added to the slide the photo of the victim, map showing the location and some clipart to represent the cash that Alvarado, the middleman, had given to the three guys.

Under each hitman's photo, she indicated their role in the killing. Under Wilson Sanchez' photo she listed that he supplied the brown Econoline van used to transport the hitmen. She added under Wilson's name the fact that he was the shooter.

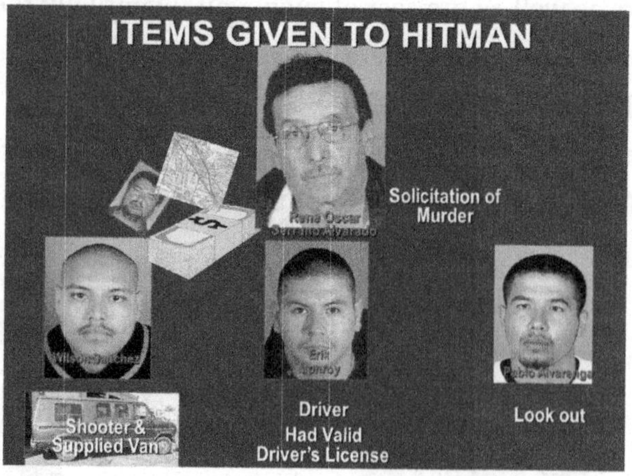

Next Beth wanted the jurors to understand where the hitmen were located in the antiquated van which they used. Although at various times they changed positions, she wanted the jurors to be able to visualize the seating arrangement in the van. The below slide illustrates where the various hitmen where located.

In order for the jurors to have a true picture of this van, Beth wanted the jurors to see this 'bucket of bolts' that Wilson Sanchez took pride in claiming as his. From the below photos the jurors could see the interior of the van. They could better understand the condition of the van and why it leaked power-steering fluid and radiator fluid.

VAN USED BY WILSON SANCHEZ

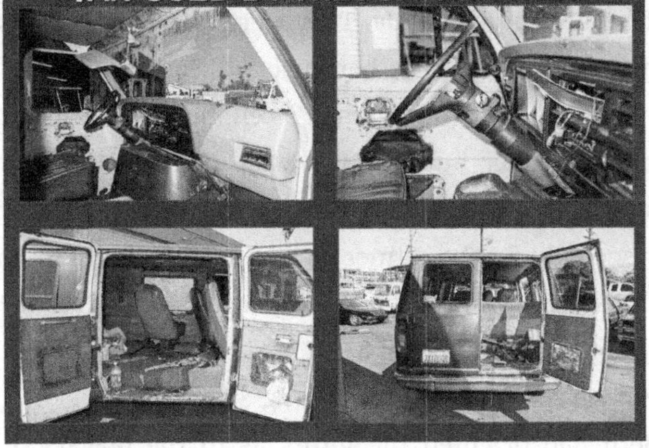

Next, Beth wanted to explain the connection between the hitmen. Both Erik Monroy and Pablo Alvarenga were longtime friends of Wilson Sanchez and they all lived in the same area of South-Central. Alvarado, the middleman, had told the hitmen that the victim-husband came home from work around 10:00 p.m.

In order to prepare for the shooting, the hitmen drove to Pablo's house to pick up a dark hoodie and some dark clothing. Then they drove to Yoda's house in the City of Compton to obtain a gun. They were told that the gun may not be operable so Pablo test-fired the weapon and determined that it did work.

By then Beth had set the stage for the jurors to comprehend the shooting. She next explained that the hitmen made two trips to the crime scene. On their first trip, they learned that the husband had already come home. Since there was no way to get the victim to come out of the house, the hitmen returned to South-Central L.A. When they arrived at Alvarado's apartment, Wilson approached Alvarado and claimed he had done the job and demanded the money. Then Alvarado contacted the wife and found out that her husband had not been shot.

Wilson admitted that they hadn't shot the victim because there was no way to get him to come outside. They were told to return to Sun Valley and this time the wife would have her husband leave the house. In order to do this, they were given the middleman's cellphone so they could call the wife to get her to have her husband leave the house. With the cellphone the hitmen made a second trip out to Sun Valley to shoot the victim.

On this second trip the hitmen had to stop to purchase gas for the van. While at the service station the three hitmen decided that Wilson Sanchez should pay both Erik and Pablo $500 for their participation in the shooting. That left Wilson receiving the remaining $7000.

After Beth had oriented the jurors as to the players in the case, she started to explain the crime scene. Since there were two streets involved, she needed the jurors to understand that the shooting occurred on Stagg Street and that the Mercedes came to rest in the middle of the street as seen on the slide below.

The other street the jurors needed to be familiar with was Arcola Avenue which was the street where the van was parked just before the shooting. The next slide showed where the vehicles were positioned on Stagg Street and the van on Arcola Avenue.

Also, this slide showed where the key eyewitness Sally Talles (pseudonym) made her observations. This was important that the jurors could visualize where this eyewitness saw the van and a person running toward the van from where the shots were fired. Beth told the jury that this witness observed where the Ford Econoline van was parked just before the shooting. She would tell the jury that she heard several gunshots and got out of her car and ducked for cover. From that position she could see a hooded male figure running from the area of the gunshots.

At the same time, she saw the brown van move forward into the intersection and the person who was running jumped in. The van turned onto Stagg Street and raced past her house. While it did, she got a good look at the van's driver's side and rear. Although she couldn't make out the parties in the van, she was able to notice that the van had a white piece of plastic or paper covering the window behind the driver's seat.

Beth went on to tell the jury that this witness would later identify the van from photos that the detectives showed her. By this time the prosecutor had carefully watched the body language of the jurors. By their expressions she felt that the jurors understood the facts leading up to the shooting of the victim.

CHAPTER 29-OPENING STATEMENT ABOUT CRIME

Next Beth began discussing what evidence the detectives had uncovered showing who was involved in this Murder. She started out by saying that officers from the LAPD North Hollywood Division responded to the crime scene after receiving several 9-1-1 calls of shots fired. Beth explained that the first responding officer would testify to discovering the victim, Reynaldo Quijano, who appeared lifeless. The officer also noticed that he was seated behind the steering wheel and the car's engine was still running with the headlights on.

The car was parked perpendicular to the curb across from the victim's house. The officer related seeing four 9mm spent casings next to the driver's side of the car. Also, the detectives recovered a gas bill on the street where the eyewitness claimed she saw the van parked just before the shooting. The gas bill was in the name of Cecilia Avila at 202 E. 47th Street, Los Angeles (Pseudonym).

Beth continued to tell the jurors that later undercover detectives set up a surveillance of that address listed on the gas bill. Over a period of several days they observed a brown Ford van being driven to and from the address. Later they determined that the driver had been Wilson Sanchez and, on several occasions, he was accompanied by Pablo Alvarenga.

Beth used the below slide to convey all that evidence to the jury. On that slide she had superimposed the gas bill with a DMV photo of the person listed on it. Behind the gas bill was the house listed on the gas bill. Directly below the photo of the house was the photo of the brown van which was parked on the street.

Also, overlaid on the van was the photo of the eyewitness who had described the window of the van which was covered with a white covering of some type.

Since the brown van was crucial to the case, Beth didn't want the jurors to be confused as to who owned and who used the van. On the next slide she placed on the left side a photo of the registered owner who was Wilson Sanchez' stepfather. On the other side of the slide Beth had a photo of Wilson Sanchez the user of the van.

CHAPTER 30- OPENING STATEMENT DEFENDANTS' STORIES

Then Beth shifted her Opening Statement to discuss the stories that the defendant, Maria Quijano, had told the detectives. The below slide was one of several in which Beth wanted the jurors to see how the defendant's statements continued to change over time. Initially the defendant claimed she didn't know that her husband had come home. She went on to claim that she was sound asleep when the shooting occurred. She claimed that she didn't hear the shooting or the sirens from vehicles responding to the shooting.

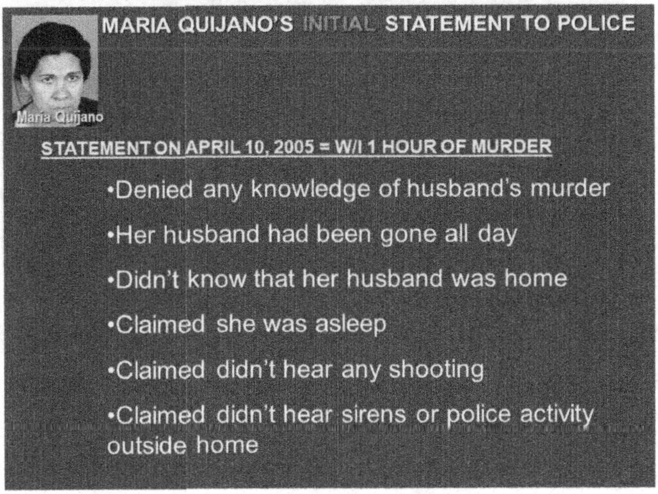

Every time the police came up with new evidence, Maria would modify her story to fit the new facts. Later the detectives spoke with the defendant's daughter who indicated that she had seen the victim's car parked out in front of the house. She even believed that she heard the victim in the master bedroom. Further the daughter stated that she fell asleep and was awakened around 12:15 a.m. by hearing the gunshots. Afterwards she heard her mother quieting the dogs and she assumed everything was all right and that was when she went back to sleep.

It was highly probative that the defendant was continuing to lie to the detectives. Beth wanted the jurors to see how Maria eventually admitted she only wanted her husband to be beat up, however she readily admitted she had discussed how much it would cost to have her husband killed.

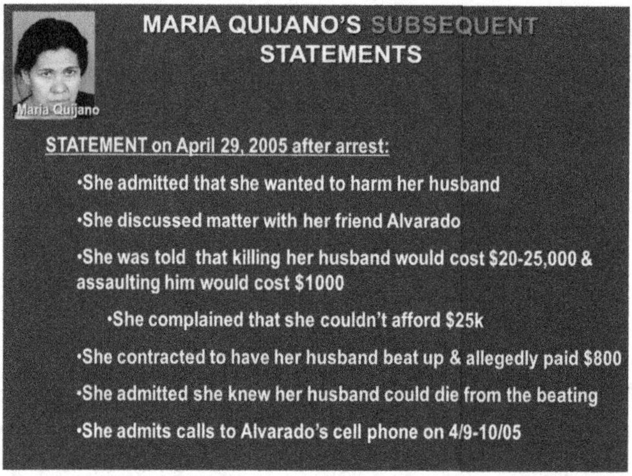

After discussing the defendant's statements, Beth knew that some of the jurors might believe Maria's claim that she didn't intend to have her husband killed. At this point Beth wanted the jurors to hear about what really happened from two of the other defendants who were also co-conspirators.

The next slide that Beth projected on the screen was that of Pablo Alvarenga with an outline to what he would be testifying to. The prosecutor explained that this witness was arrested on May 19, 2005, and shortly thereafter he gave a statement to the detectives. Beth summarized his statement by saying that it isn't unusual for a criminal to initially lie to the detectives. She went on explaining to the jury that Pablo had given several different versions as to what happened and each time, he downplayed his involvement.

Pablo didn't want to implicate his pal Erik Monroy. It wasn't until December 12, 2006, that Pablo was willing to provide a complete description of what everyone did the night of the shooting.

Beth explained to the jury that Pablo finally laid out what really happened. He told the detectives that the three of them made two trips to the victim's house. On the first trip the victim had already come home so there was no way he could be shot. On the second trip Alvarado gave the guys his cellphone so they could contact the wife to have her send her husband outside. Pablo explained how Wilson approached the victim who was seated in his car and shot him several times.

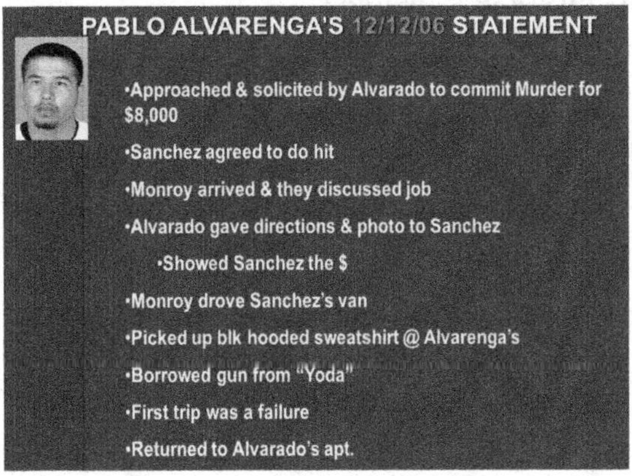

Beth indicated that this witness Pablo would describe how Wilson returned and obtained the $8,000 from Alvarado. After that Wilson paid both Pablo and Erik $500 for their assistance in the shooting.

The above slide was used by the prosecutor to show what Pablo would be testifying to. Beth wanted to lay the foundation for why the jurors should believe Pablo. She was very direct with the jurors by telling them that for his truthful and complete testimony, Pablo was allowed to enter a guilty plea to Voluntary Manslaughter and receive a sentence of 22 years in state prison.

Without missing a beat, Beth went on to her next co-conspirator witness who was Erik Monroy. Some six months after the murder, the detectives interviewed Erik and he admitted that on April 9th, he had run into Wilson and Pablo and learned about an old guy asking someone to kill a person out in the San Fernando Valley. Beth told the jury that Erik would describe to them exactly how he drove the van to Sun Valley. There Wilson got out of the van and shot this man who was in his car. Afterwards they returned to South-Central where Wilson received the $8,000 and gave $500 to both him and Pablo.

The prosecutor wanted the jurors to thoroughly understand Erik Monroy's testimony so she used the below slide to illustrate the key points she wanted the jurors to remember.

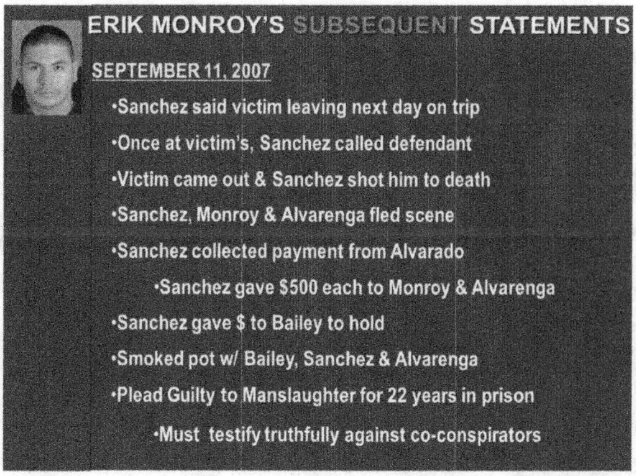

Beth knew that Erik Monroy would be a stronger witness than Pablo Alvarenga. So, it was imperative that the jurors understand Erik's testimony. When she finished explaining what she expected this witness to testify to, she reminded the jury that Erik was also given a plea bargain permitting him to plead guilty to Voluntary Manslaughter and receive 22 years in state prison. She stressed that agreement was based on him testifying truthfully otherwise he would be prosecuted for MURDER which could mean that he would receive a sentence of life in prison.

By the end of her Opening Statement, Beth wanted to summarize for the jurors as to who was involved in the conspiracy to kill the victim. She reused the below slide so the jury could see all the parties who played a role in the Conspiracy to Commit Murder.

During the prosecutor's Opening Statement, the expression on several of the jurors' faces turned from quizzical to solemn. All of a sudden, these jurors realized that they were going to be called upon to determine who was telling the truth. Should they believe the defendant-wife or believe two of the co-conspirators? This wasn't going to be an open-and-shut case handed to them on a silver platter.

Beth left up on the screen the last slide showing all the co-conspiracy within a circle. In a somber and convincing voice, she said, "This defendant engaged in a conspiracy with Oscar Alvarado to find someone to kill her husband. He just did that when he contacted Wilson Sanchez to conspire with Pablo Alvarenga and Erik Monroy to carry out the hit for a specified amount of money."

The prosecutor moved away from the lectern and stepped to the side being directly in front of the jurors. She paused for a moment and said, "I will have the opportunity to discuss the evidence that will be presented to you and the law that applies." Then she raised her head so she could scan the eyes of all the jurors and with a firm and confident voice she said, "I will ask you to find this defendant, the wife, guilty of the charges and the alleged allegations."

Then Beth slowly turned slightly to her side and waited a moment to see if the full impact of her Opening Statement had sunk in with all the jurors. She uttered the words, "Thank you for your attention" as she returned to the counsel table and sat down in her assigned DA's chair.

Her presentation was arranged like a conductor directing a hundred-piece orchestra. She had gotten everyone's attention and kept the jurors spellbound. But the great unknown was whether her key witnesses would be able to deliver and testify in a consistent manner.

Next the Defense attorney stood up and went to the lectern and started a conciliatory Opening Statement. He stressed that it wouldn't be fair to his client if they were swayed by what the prosecutor had said since that wasn't evidence. He asked the jurors to reserve judgment until all the evidence had been presented to them. Several of the jurors slightly nodded their heads as if they hadn't been moved by what Beth had just laid' out to them.

The Defense attorney knew that his case wasn't going to be won on the basis of the Defense witnesses he would be calling to testify. His entire case would rest on his litigation skills of cross-examining the prosecution witnesses. The Defense attorney understood that if he could attack the credibility of the two co-conspirators' testimony, he could create some level of reasonable doubt which would allow his client, the wife, to dodge the bullet of a conviction.

That concluded the Opening Statements from both sides and then it was time for the trial to begin. The big question was whether the prosecutor could actually prove up everything, she had told the jury?

CHAPTER 31- TRIAL

The prosecution's first witness was Tony Herrera who was the defendant's son. Earlier during the pretrial stage, Beth had difficulty finding him in order to talk to him. Obviously, this witness didn't want to say or do anything that might be detrimental to his mother's case. He certainly didn't want to be helpful for the prosecution. Beth realized that she had a dicey situation in calling him as a witness when she didn't know exactly what he would say in court.

Beth decided to take a non-confrontational approach with the defendant's son by asking him general questions which elicited non-threatening information. She got him to explain that his mother, the defendant, had been married to the victim, Reynaldo, for 12 years and they lived as a couple in the house at 7737 Arcola, Sun Valley. Also, he testified that his mother had mentioned to him that she suspected her husband, Reynaldo, was having an affair. He went on to say that his half-sister, Dorthey lived in the house as well as another couple who rented one of the back bedrooms.

This witness, Tony Herrera, explained that Reynaldo would visit relatives in El Salvador twice a year. He knew that Reynaldo was to leave for El Salvador the next morning. His mother had called him asking him to drop off his keys to his Cadillac which was parked in the driveway. When Reynaldo traveled out of the country, he would leave his big truck parked in the driveway. Tony testified that when he was dropping off the keys, he noticed Reynaldo's brown Mercedes parked in front of the house.

The jurors must have wondered what all this moving of vehicles in the driveway had to do with this Murder case. After several minutes of softball questions, Beth shifted to what she was really after. Then Beth asked about large sums of money that his mother had withdrawn from her bank account. The witness claimed it was for the down payment for a condo he was attempting to purchase. Beth wasn't so concerned about what he claimed the money was for but she wanted the jury to be aware that his mother, the defendant, had access to large amounts of money.

As an experienced litigator, Beth knew that calling the defendant's son as her first witness wasn't the best way to start the presentation of evidence. However, since it was the first day of the trial the defendant's son happened to be in the courtroom. Beth wanted to take advantage of this situation since she didn't know if she could ever get him back to testify in court.

She finished up quickly with the defendant's son and moved on to her next witness. Then she called Ernest Sellers to the witness stand and he established exactly when the shooting occurred. He testified that at 12:12 a.m. on April 10, 2005, he heard shots fired. Since he was working on his computer, he could be precise as to the time of the shooting.

The testimony of Mr. Sellers was short and next Beth called the Medical Examiner from the Coroner's Office. His testimony wasn't earthshaking since he merely testified that the victim's death was due to gunshot wounds to his torso. He said that the gunshot wounds were consistent with someone who was seated in a vehicle.

Beth got the medical examiner to elaborate that one bullet entered the left nipple area and exited the body on the right side. Another bullet entered the left lung and traveled through to the right lung. Other bullets hit the left armpit and left wrist. Also, he explained that one of the victim's wounds showed stippling and soot on the clothing. He stated that meant that the shooter had to be firing the handgun within inches of the victim.

After calling these three peripheral witnesses, Beth was ready to set the stage for the jurors. In order to frame the picture of the crime scene Beth called the officer who was first to arrive. **Officer Michael Higgins** took the witness stand and laid out what he observed. He indicated that he arrived at the crime scene at 12:25 a.m. The first thing he noticed was a Mercedes in the middle of the street. Then he exited his police car and approached the Mercedes, which had its engine running with the headlights on.

The officer explained to the jury that he saw a male seated in the driver's seat who didn't seemed to be moving. He shined his flashlight on the driver to get a better look and he could see that the person appeared to have been shot. The driver's side window had been shot out and shards of glass were everywhere. When he was able to view the interior of the Mercedes, he could see that the car was still in 'Drive.' He explained to the jury how he rendered the vehicle safe by turning off the ignition. Then he used his fingers to try to find a pulse on the victim without any success.

Next the officer related to the jury that he cordoned off the crime scene. While doing this he noticed a piece of paper in the street. He went over to it and picked it up and tried to figure out what it was. After looking at it, he was able to determine that it was a gas bill for a residence in South-Central LA. He testified that he told the patrol sergeant that he found this gas bill.

Detective Joe Espinosa was called next and he testified to finding the four expended shell casings next to the Mercedes. They all appeared to be in a row indicating that the shooter may have been running or at least moving while doing the shooting. Since no firearm was ever recovered the shell casing couldn't be matched to any particular weapon.

Often shell casings become the connecting evidence to a case. However, Beth wasn't going to have the opportunity to rely on ballistic evidence to prove her case. She was going to have to prove this case based on old-fashioned gumshoe police work.

CHAPTER 32 WITNESS SALLY TALLES

Beth was looking forward to calling the eyewitness, Sally Talles. The prosecutor knew that the jurors would like her since she was one of those witnesses who jurors didn't have to wonder if they were telling the truth. This witness wasn't identifying any one of the defendants as being involved. All she was doing was fingering the van that was used as the getaway vehicle. Since Wilson was the user of that vehicle, he was indirectly connected to the shooting even though she couldn't positively identify him as the shooter.

Beth wanted the jurors to be fully impressed with her testimony so she slowed down the tempo of her questioning. First, she had Miss Talles refer to a poster board showing a map of the crime scene. The witness pointed out where she had been parked and where she saw the van parked on Arcola Avenue. The witness said, "As I pulled up—as I was on the phone. I had parked my car. And I told the person I was having a conversation with that I would call them back once I got inside."

She went on to say, "I was opening the door and I heard three gunshots so then when I heard them, I looked to see where they were coming from. And I remember having the sound draw my attention to the intersection of Arcola and Stagg. And I ran because I got scared. And as I was running, I saw someone—it's kind of hard to see—someone coming from the direction of the intersection."

Beth glanced at the jurors and could see that they were intently listening to every word the witness spoke. Beth wished all of her witnesses could be as impressive in front of the jury. Next Beth turned the questioning to the location of the van. Sally Talles said, "There was something weird that caught my attention right away. As I was coming down the street before I even parked, I noticed there was a van parked in the red zone underneath a street light and no one ever parks there."

Miss Talles went on to say, "It's a red zone. No one parks there because we all kind of have our parking spots and no one ever parks there because it's a red zone and this light is the only one in that whole intersection so you would see something unusual right away."

Beth wanted to sear into the jurors' psyches the fact that this witness was being truthful and had an excellent memory of what she saw on the night of the shooting. Beth asked another question about the neighborhood to cement in the mind of the jurors that this was a witness they could rely on. The witness replied, "We all are very familiar with each other and with our vehicles because whenever there is something that is out of place someone always brings it to the attention of the other neighbors. This is a pretty safe area so whenever we see something that is unusual everyone notices."

Then Beth wanted this witness to testify to why she could remember the van so well. The witness went on to say, "It was a dark-colored van that was parked in the red underneath the street light where no one ever parks and it had an unusual white or light-colored covering over the driver's side rear window."

Further she stated, "It was a dark color. Either brown or black. I remember I initially had thought it was black because I was so nervous when I was running to hide it just looked like a dark-colored van but the one thing that was so clear about that night and that I remember distinctly is a white or light covering over the window."

Now it was time to have this witness explain who she saw. "I saw someone running from—I don't know my directions very well but from—farther down Stagg Street where it's straight ahead. This person was wearing a hooded sweatshirt which was black in color." When asked if she could identify that person the witness said, "It looked like a male by the build of the body. I couldn't see the face. But for sure it looked like a male by the build of the body." She went on to describe the person by saying, "I figured in their twenties maybe late twenties, early twenties. Just because of the way they were dressed and way that they were running".

Beth had to think to herself that this was one case where it was helpful that the witness couldn't identify the suspects. This witness was so truthful in her testimony that she honestly couldn't identify anyone. All the prosecution needed from this witness was the fact that she could positively identify the van as the getaway vehicle used by the hitmen.

Beth finished up with this witness by having her explain how they escaped. "I saw the van pull into the intersection as I noticed the person running, I saw the van pulling into the intersection that was parked in the red curb to the intersection of Stagg and Arcola. The person who was running to the intersection got into the passenger side door and then the van proceeded down Stagg Street." "I couldn't see the person. I know that someone was driving that van because the other person got in on the passenger side."

Then Beth asked her about the other car in which the victim had been shot. She related the following, "The vehicle was on Stagg Street parked perpendicular to the street. It was a black sedan. And I could see a body crouched over the steering wheel. I could see a body there and it wasn't moving. When I called 911, I told them that the headlights were on the vehicle and that the person inside didn't seem to be moving."

She went on to testify that, "Yes, I went to my room in the house and called 911 and I was looking out the blinds at the vehicle to see if it would move. I told them that I had heard gunshots and that someone had been shot, that the vehicle had the lights on and the person didn't seem to be moving."

Lastly Beth asked this witness if she later identified the van from photos that the detectives showed her. She continued by saying, "They showed me several pictures of different types of vans and colors. And I pointed to the brown van with the white cover over the window and told them that I could identify that one as the one that I had seen that night. The other picture was of a silver minivan and I knew it was not a minivan. It was a cargo van like a passenger van, not a small minivan. I explained that it was an older van with that white covering over the window. That was the one thing that stuck in my head."

Beth was sorry she was finished with such a strong positive and credible witness. She could see from the expression on the jurors faces they totally loved her. Then Beth looked at the judge and said, "I have no further questions for this witness." At that point the judge turned to the Defense attorney and asked, "Do you wish to cross-exam this witness?"

The Defense attorney jumped up and walked to the lectern and started asking questions. He started asking her about whether she remembered seeing the rear of the van. She stated that she told the detectives that she only saw lights going around the corner. The Defense attorney thought he could trip up this witness. He said, "What did you tell the police?" Her answer was, "I initially told them no because the only thing that I remembered were lights going around the corner."

The Defense attorney pounced on this by saying, "Okay. Did you at the preliminary hearing testify under oath that you purposely omitted things during the interview with the detectives because you didn't want to be involved?" She nodded and said, "Initially I didn't." Then the Defense attorney felt he had made the witness look untruthful and he said, "And you didn't tell them everything because you were scared?"

The witness Sally Talles responded, "Yes, when you see something like that happen—The reason I hid was because I figured if they saw me, I was going to get killed, too. I was going to get shot at, too." The Defense attorney wanted to make this witness look like a liar and he asked, "What was the reason for not telling the police that you saw the back of the van?" Her response was, "The only thing I saw from the back of the van was the lights going around the corner. I didn't see doors. I didn't see a license plate. I didn't see anything else."

The Defense attorney must have thought that he had scored a major attack on her credibility. All this witness was telling the jurors was that she was scared to death and didn't want to get involved in something that could be harmful to her. More likely the jurors were more favorably impressed with this witness and the Defense attorney most likely didn't erode her credibility one bit.

CHAPTER 33- ERIK MONROY TESTIMONY

The prosecutor would like all her future witnesses to be as good as Sally Talles. But the real world is paved with difficult witnesses and those who have considerable baggage they carry with them when they take the witness stand. Beth called as her next witness "Erik Monroy." She knew that her case would be won or lost depending on how well he testified before the jury.

Beth knew that the Defense attorney would try to crucify this witness on cross-examination. The Defense would paint Erik Monroy as a witness who was willing to say anything in order to obtain a more lenient sentence for himself. As we have discussed when the DA gives either leniency or immunity to a witness, the Defense will have a field day in trying to show that this witness isn't believable. The Defense will paint a picture that the witness will say anything to save its own neck.

Beth knew there were two approaches as to how to present such a witness to the jury. One approach was to wait until the end of the witness's testimony to mention to the jury that he or she had received a plea bargain. Another approach was to start the direct examination by spelling out the plea bargain the witness has been given in order to testify.

Beth is one of those prosecutors who wants to be upfront and tell the jury that a deal has been made. She started out with the first question being as follows:

"In this case, sir, did you plead guilty to a violation of Penal Code section 192, that being the crime of Voluntary Manslaughter?" Erik Monroy sat in the witness chair and looked at the prosecutor and stated in a contrite voice, "Yes mama." Beth went on to say, "And for that plea of guilty you will receive a sentence of twenty-two years." The witnesses answered in the affirmative. Beth further asked, "Do you understand today that you're testifying under a grant of immunity? And that immunity does not cover you if you were to lie on the stand and commit perjury?" Again, the witness answered with a strong, "Yes."

Beth went on to say, "Do you understand that it will be the judge who determines whether you lied in this case?" Again, the witness nodded and replied "Yes." (In this case the term 'immunity' was used since technically he was being given immunity from prosecution for the charge of Murder. However, in the process he was being given a more 'lenient' sentence.)

Beth liked to get the bad news out before going into what she wanted the jurors to remember. Then she looked up at her witness and started firing off her questions. First, she wanted Erik to explain how he knew Wilson Sanchez. That was when he explained that he and Wilson lived in the same apartment house and had known each other for over three years. He knew that Wilson drove an old brown van which his stepfather had given him. When she asked Erik about the van, he didn't hesitate in saying that it had a covered window on the driver's side. He said that the van was very recognizable.

Then the next question was about the friends that he hung out with. He mentioned that Pablo Alvarenga was another close acquaintance of both him and Wilson. At this point Beth wanted to clear the air about the inaccurate statements he made to the detectives. Erik freely admitted that he lied about what had happened since he didn't want to get in trouble and he wanted to protect his buddies Pablo, Wilson and Will. When asked who was Will, he said that it was Willis Barnes.

Beth had established that all these guys knew each other and hung out together. Then she knew it was time to start laying out the facts leading up to the shooting. She asked Erik what did he do on April 9th, 2005. Sometimes with such an open-ended question the attorney gets more then he or she wants. Erik was under tremendous pressure to tell the entire truth and nothing but the truth. So, in his mind he started from the beginning. He stated that he got up at six o'clock in the evening and took a shower and got dressed and left his place. He rode his bike all the way to 84th Street.

There he saw Tweedy and Tony Touch seated in a white Honda. He rode his bike up to their car and started talking to them. From there he went into the building on the corner and saw Wilson and Pablo talking to this old guy. Once they were finished with their discussion, he went over to Pablo and asked what was going on. Pablo had a strange expression on his face as though he couldn't believe something he had heard. Pablo took a deep breath and tried to explain what the old guy had told him. He said that the old guy had approached him and asked him if he would kill some guy for $8,000.

Erik told the jury that he was surprised by this statement. Then he noticed the old guy walk back into his apartment as Wilson approached Erik and Pablo. Erik testified, "Wilson came and showed us a picture and a piece of paper with the address, the directions how to get to the place to go kill that guy. That's when he told me—that's when Wilson told me the old guy was giving him eight thousand to go kill this guy and he showed us a picture and paper with the directions on there. He said he's going to be driving a brown Mercedes and he got to be there at nine in the night and guy had to be killed that night, the same night."

Beth wanted to slow down Erik's testimony since it was crucial that the jurors understand all these details. Beth asked Erik what was Wilson Sanchez' reaction. Erik said, "Yes, he said that he was going to go kill this guy." Then Erik explained how he got involved. "He asked me to drive his brown van." Beth asked Erik the simple question which was, "Did you agree to drive the van?" Erik's response was, "I felt peer pressure when he asked me because I told him no and he was like are you going to let me down and I was like, fuck it, let's go, so we went."

It had to be hard for Erik to discuss all this in front of the jury. It made him out as a weak person who couldn't say no to something that was causing him to serve 22 years of his life in prison. If only he had walked away his life would have been entirely different.

Beth didn't want Erik to become unraveled thinking about his tragic mistake. She started asking about the hoodie that they picked up from Pablo's place. Then next Erik testified to driving down to Compton to pick up a gun from Yoda.

Erik testified, "Wilson told Yoda that he needed a gun so Yoda gave him a 9-millimeter but warned him that it might not work. We went around the block. Pablo put the gun outside the van and he pulled the trigger and it shot once up in the air. After the test firing, he went to the back of the van and put the gun away in some little wood panel that pops open." Wilson had been driving when they went to Compton. After they had picked up the gun Wilson stopped the van and told Erik that he wanted him to drive since he was the only one who had a valid driver's license. Wilson's explanation was since they had a gun in the vehicle, he wanted someone who had a driver's license to be driving if they got stopped by the cops.

Erik then described to the jury that he didn't know where he was to go. Wilson was seated next to him on the passenger side and he was staring at the directions that the old guy had handed him. He drove the old van up the 110 Freeway until he got to the downtown interchange where he headed north on the 101 Freeway. All that Erik remembered was that they eventually found the location in Sun Valley.

They pulled over and waited. Wilson looked around to get his bearing. After waiting for a while Wilson announced that the he could see the brown Mercedes. Then there was a long silence to collect their thoughts as to what to do. They were hoping that the victim would come out of the house and get back into the Mercedes. As the minutes drew longer these less-than-professional hitmen decided to give up and return to their hangout at 84th Street.

When they got back to Alvarado's apartment, Erik said, "Wilson went to the back of the van, he got the gun and he said I'll be back and he left. He went towards the old guy's house." Later Erik testified, "He told me and Pablo that he told the old guy that the job had been done, that he had killed the guy already and he wanted the money." Erik testified, "The old guy said that it hadn't taken place yet because he was supposed to get a phone call from somebody that was watching."

After Wilson's confrontation with the old guy they were all seated in the van wondering what was going to happen next. Surprisingly, Erik exclaimed that the old guy came out to the van and handed his cellphone to Wilson and told him to use it to call the wife when they had reached the location. Beth realized that Erik's testimony about the cellphone would be crucial to provide the corroboration she needed when using an accomplice. So, Beth wanted to slow down the tempo of the testimony so the jurors could have time to digest every single morsel of testimony about the borrowed cellphone.

Erik testified that Wilson told him to stop to get gas on the second trip. He saw an open service station at Figueroa and Manchester Boulevards and he pulled into the far side pumps. Erik said, "Wilson got out to go pump gas and I grabbed the cellphone and started talking to my mom. After that I called my girlfriend." Then Erik explained that when he was talking to his mom he was interrupted by an 'incoming call' which he answered. He heard a woman's voice on the line which said, "Are you going to be the one that was going to do it?"

Erik related that he told the lady, "'No.' I said hold on and I gave the phone to Wilson." Later Wilson told him that was the lady who wanted her husband killed. The reason she wanted him dead was that her husband had raped their three-year-old daughter. She went on to tell Wilson to call her as soon as they got to the Valley so she could get her husband to go outside.

This was the time that Erik had his only contact with this defendant, the wife. He continued to explain that they eventually arrived back at the house in the Valley. Since Wilson had driven from the service station to the house it was Wilson who parked the van in the red zone. Erik said that Wilson got out on the driver's side and told him to scoot over to drive the van. He saw Wilson holding the cellphone and appeared to be making the call to the wife.

Several minutes later he said, "I seen him run towards the inside of the street. Then the van was in 'park' and Erik put it into 'drive' and moved forward to the middle of the intersection. As Wilson ran up towards the brown Mercedes, he started shooting in there. The brown Mercedes was lurched forward and then stopped. Then Wilson ran back to the van."

Beth had walked Erik through all the facts leading up to the shooting. Now she wanted to finish up by explaining what happened afterwards. Erik related to the jury that he drove the van back to 84th Street and Wilson went into the old guy's place and got the money. Erik testified, "He told me that the old guy had called the lady to verify that the job was done and the lady gave him the okay for Alvarado to give the money to Wilson."

Next Beth needed to have Erik explain to the jury the other important corroboration. The prosecutor asked who else they had contact with. At that point Erik explained that they drove over to Willis Barnes's place and Wilson gave him all the money to hold for safekeeping. After that Wilson gave Erik money to get some weed, which he did. Then they went over to a city park and got high and fell asleep.

The rest of Erik's testimony was just to put the entire case in context. Beth asked Erik if he had any further contact with Wilson. He indicated that he saw Wilson two days later and he appeared to be a new man. He was now an owner of new green Camry that he was proudly driving around. He had installed a new sound system in his car. He also sported a new cellphone with new clothes. For fun he had purchased a little Ninja mini motorcycle.

Beth had gotten all the necessary evidence out of Erik but she knew that within minutes the Defense attorney would try to paint a picture that this witness Erik Monroy was nothing but a lying Judas Priest. In order to soften the attack Beth asked Erik to explain why he had previously lied to the detectives. She got him to admit that if he told the truth he knew it would get him into trouble. Also, he didn't want to implicate any of his buddies who he considered his closest friends.

Beth didn't know how well Erik would stand up under intense cross-examination. Trying to project the image that Erik might have lied in the past to protect himself and others, now he was under oath telling the full truth and nothing but the truth. The entire case was riding on how the jurors would view Erik as a witness.

CHAPTER 34- PABLO ALVARENGA TESTIMONY

The Defense's cross-examination of Erik was extensive and made some inroads in the prosecution's case. Beth thought that the Defense had been thorough but that she could repair any damage that the Defense had inflicted on Erik's testimony. She decided to start the testimony of Pablo in the same way of explaining that Pablo had received a plea bargain. She went through it step by step with Pablo admitting that if he testified to the truth that he would receive 22 years in state prison.

Beth wanted the jurors to see that this witness's incentive to tell the truth was based on the fact that if he didn't tell the truth he would be charged with Murder. Then Beth was confronted with a slight ripple as seen in her questions and Pablo's answers below.

Q. DO YOU KNOW WHAT WOULD HAPPEN TO YOU IF YOU WERE TO LIE?

A. I'LL GET CHARGED FOR THE MURDER.

Q. DO YOU KNOW WHO MAKES THE DECISION AS TO WHETHER OR NOT YOU ARE TELLING THE TRUTH ON THE STAND VERSUS LYING?

A. NO

Q. YOU DO NOT KNOW WHO THAT WOULD BE?

A. WHAT DO YOU MEAN?

Q. IF YOU LIE HERE IN COURT WHEN YOU'RE TESTIFYING DO YOU REMEMBER FROM YOUR PLEA THAT DATE THAT YOU PLED GUILTY -DO

YOU REMEMBER FROM YOUR PLEA AGREEMENT WHO MAKES THE DECISION ON WHETHER OR NOT YOU'VE TOLD THE TRUTH OR NOT?

A. YOU

Q. ME?

A. YEAH.

Q. DO YOU REMEMBER BEING TOLD THAT, IN FACT IT'S THE JUDGE?

A. NO

Q. NO, YOU DON'T REMEMBER THAT?

A. I DON'T REMEMBER

Beth took a deep breath hoping the jury hadn't noticed what this witness had just said. Just a day before, she had gone over the questioning and he seemed to be on board. How was she going to get herself out of this uncomfortable situation? Without missing a beat Beth moved on to her next question as though nothing had happened.

Q. HAVE YOU BEEN TOLD WHAT TO SAY HERE TODAY?

A. NO, MA'AM.

Q., NOW, HAVE YOU PREVIOUSLY—BEFORE THE PLEA THAT YOU ENTERED IN THIS CASE OF VOLUNTARY MANSLAUGHTER, HAVE YOU PREVIOUSLY BEEN CONVICTED OF ANOTHER CRIME?

A. YEAH ROBBERY.

Q. DO YOU KNOW SOMEBODY BY THE NAME OF WILSON SANCHEZ?

A. YES, MA'AM.

Beth knew that as much preparation she had done for this case, there was no guarantee that her witnesses would answer as planned. In previous discussions with the accomplices, she knew that Erik was the sharper of the two. Since Pablo couldn't keep straight the plea bargain, she now knew that this witness wasn't going to be an easy 'walk in the park.'

Beth had Pablo testify about knowing Wilson Sanchez and having ridden in his old brown van. Beth realized that she needed to question Pablo at a slower pace so he wouldn't become confused. But she wasn't ready for the bumpy ride her questioning of Pablo would become. An example was as follows:

Q. BETWEEN THE TWO OF THEM, WILSON SANCHEZ AND ERIK MONROY, WHICH OF THE TWO OF THEM WOULD YOU SAY YOU WERE CLOSER TO?

A. ERIK

Q. YOU WERE CLOSER TO ERIK?

A. (HE NODDED HIS HEAD)

Q. DO YOU REMEMBER TELLING US INITIALLY THAT YOU WERE CLOSER TO WILSON?

A. NO.

Beth had to wonder why witnesses have to fall apart when they are testifying in front of a jury. She was glad that she had called Erik first, since he had a better grasp as to how to testify. Pablo was going to be a challenging witness not able to stay on script.

Beth asked Pablo what did the old man say to him. Pablo testified, "He said that he was looking for someone to kill someone. He was going to pay—he was looking for someone so he could pay to kill someone for $8,000." He related that Wilson and Erik came up later and asked what the old guy was doing. Pablo said, "He was looking for someone to kill someone." Wilson went over to the old guy and asked him if he was serious. The man said it had to be done by today by eight or nine o'clock.

Pablo further related, "Wilson asked him if he had a picture of him or anything and the guy said yeah. And then they walked across the street and I followed them. We walked up to it and the old guy opened the driver's side door and he went under the seat and he took out a clear zip-lock baggie and it had papers and gloves in it and he was looking for the picture but he didn't find it. Then the old guy said it must be in his house and he crossed over the street to his apartment."

Within minutes he returned with a photo of the person to be killed. Wilson held the photo and carefully reviewed it and handed it back. Then Pablo testified, "Wilson asked him if he had the money and the old guy said, yeah, it was in his house. And he says I want to see it and the old guy said no because his wife was in the house. And he said now you want me to believe you—now you want me to believe that you got the money."

It seemed that the negotiation for the Contract Killing had hit a snag. Then Pablo spelled out what happened next. "I guess he thought about it and he was like, all right, then let's go. And after that both of them walked across the street and went into the old guy's apartment." Pablo was able to describe what really happened as he explained, "He said that he had the money and he was going to do it but he needed a gun and he was going to get one from one of our friends."

Apparently, Pablo was getting tired of all the questioning and started the 'amnesia routine' of not remembering. Beth was stuck in a difficult situation. She didn't want to come down hard on Pablo especially in front of the jury. Now she used a firm voice when asking Pablo to remember certain statement he had made in the DA's Office during his proffered statement. It went as follows:

Q. DO YOU REMEMBER BEING ASKED IF YOU HAD TOLD TWEEDY AND TONY TOUCH ABOUT THE FACT THAT THE OLD GUY WANTED YOU GUYS TO GO KILL SOMEBODY?

A. YEA. I THINK—YEAH.

Q. DO YOU REMEMBER WHEN I ASKED YOU DID YOU TELL THOSE GUYS ABOUT WHAT HAD HAPPENED YOU SAID, YEAH, THEY KNEW ABOUT IT?

DO YOU REMEMBER THAT?

A. YES.

Q. DO YOU REMEMBER SAYING I THINK IT WAS ME AND ERIK. WE HAD TOLD THEM BECAUSE THEY WERE LOOKING FOR WEED.

DO YOU REMEMBER THAT?

A. YES

Q. DO YOU REMEMBER SAYING TO ERIK THAT HE HAD TOLD THEM ABOUT IT?

A. I FORGOT ABOUT THAT. THEY KNEW WHAT WAS GOING ON?

Q. DO YOU REMEMBER SAYING THAT WE HAD TOLD THEM ABOUT WHAT THE GUY HAD WANTED. WE HAD TOLD THEM.

A. YEAH.

Q. AND DO YOU REMEMBER ME ASKING YOU THAT HE WANTED YOU GUYS TO GO KILL SOMEBODY AND YOUR ANSWER WAS THAT HE WANTED. YEAH?

A. YEAH.

Q. THE QUESTION BEING YOU HAD TOLD TONY AND TWEEDY THAT AND YOUR ANSWER, YEAH, SO THEY BASICALLY KNEW WHAT WAS GOING ON.

DO YOU REMEMBER THAT?

A. YEAH.

Q. IS THAT ACCURATE?

DOES THAT REFRESH YOUR RECOLLECTION?

A. YEAH.

Beth had to wonder why was her own witness making everything so difficult. Was he doing this on purpose or not? Then she decided to move on and asked the basic question as to when all three of the hitmen talked about doing the hit together. This seemed to be a simple question but the following is what occurred before the jury.

Q. NOW, I'M ASSUMING AT SOME POINT BEFORE YOU GOT IN THE VAN FROM 84TH STREET THAT YOU HAD SOME CONVERSATION.

DID YOU AND WILSON AND ERIK DISCUSS WHETHER OR NOT YOU WERE GOING TO GO WITH WILSON?

A. NO. I DON'T REMEMBER, NO.

Q. ONCE WILSON CAME BACK AND SAID HE WAS GOING TO GO TO YODA'S TO GET THE GUN DID YOU DECIDE TO GO WITH HIM?

A. YES.

Q. WHAT ABOUT ERIK? DID HE ALSO GO WITH YOU?

A. YEA.

Q. WAS THERE A CONVERSATION BEFORE HE GOT INTO THE VAN ABOUT GOING WITH HIM?

A. NO HE WAS STILL OUTSIDE.

Q. AT ANY POINT IN TIME DID WILSON TALK TO YOU AND ERIK ABOUT WHAT HE WANTED YOU TO DO?

A. NO.

Q. DID HE ASK YOU TO GO WITH HIM?

A. NO.

Q. DID HE ASK ERIK TO GO WITH HIM?

A. I DON'T REMEMBER THAT.

Q. BUT YOU JUMPED IN?

A. YEAH.

Beth had to retain her composure. But why was this witness not cooperating? These are the times prosecutors wonder why after graduating from law school that they didn't take a job with a prestigious law firm. Beth knew that making her witness look like a jerk wasn't going to help her case in front of the jurors. She bit her tongue and pretended everything was fine when she asked Pablo if they stopped at his house to get a hoodie sweatshirt for Wilson.

After the question about the hoodie, Beth asked Pablo about picking up the gun from Yoda. Pablo explained that they got a nine-millimeter handgun from Yoda. Pablo said, "That he (Yoda) wasn't sure the gun worked. He said that it got stuck one time when he shot it. Then he went outside and—he wanted us to shoot it on the side of his house. Well, Wilson was going to shoot it and Yoda said better not do it—we better go down the block because I think his mom was in the front. Then we just left and we went around the block and that's when we test-fired it."

The questions about the gun went well and Beth started asking what they did when they reached the house in the Valley. Pablo said, "We went past the house and then parked. We were waiting. And we seen the car show up. We seen a car show up. And Wilson turned on the car to go over there. Before he was like he wanted just to shoot—drive up and to shoot him. He was telling us what should he do and stuff. And we turned around and Erik went straight when he was supposed to turn. Wilson had told him to turn near where the guy was."

Pablo went on to say, "He (Wilson) was saying, stupid, why did you go that way. He was telling him (Erik) why are you going that way and we went around the block and we came back and the guy was parked. And I guess the guy had went in the house." Pablo went on to explain that they waited maybe thirty minutes hoping he would come out. When nothing happened, they decided to return to 84th Street.

Next Pablo explained to the jury how Wilson was going to scam the old guy by telling him that the job had been done. He testified, "He (Wilson) said he was going to go and tell the old guy that he did it and he said if he didn't give him the money that he was going to scare him with the gun." Pablo went on to explain that Wilson went into the old guy's apartment and told him that he killed the victim. Both Wilson and the old guy came back to the van and got in. Pablo said, "They got in the car. Then Wilson asked me—He was like didn't I shoot the guy. And I was like 'Yeah.' And the old guy said, no you didn't. He said, no, you didn't because he said he was talking to the lady right now and that she says she was in the bathroom. She says she was in the bathroom there and that her husband was asleep."

The charade wasn't working as Pablo said, "I think the lady had told him on the phone that—to send us over there again because she was going to tell the guy to—she was going to send the guy to go get something like milk or soda from the store." Then Pablo indicated that it was agreed that the old guy would loan his cellphone to Wilson so he could call her when they had returned. Upon their return to the house Wilson called the lady on the old man's phone.

Within five minutes a man came out and got into the Mercedes. Then Pablo described how the shooting occurred by testifying, "He (Wilson) gets out and then I remember—I don't know if he ran or walked over there but he went towards the victim and I remember hearing gunshots and when the gunshots—when he shot, Erik pulled up in the middle of the block and after that Wilson came back running. He hopped in the van."

Shortly thereafter "Wilson got a phone call on the cellphone and he said that the lady said that it was done and that when he got there to tell him that it was done and that when he got there to tell the old guy to call—to call her so he could release the money." When they got back to the old guys apartment, Wilson received the $8,000 for doing the killing. Pablo said that Wilson and Erik counted all the cash and it came up $20.00 short. Wilson was upset being shorted and wanted to confront the old guy over the shortage. Both Erik and Pablo told him to forget it and accept what he had gotten.

Beth was finishing up with Pablo's direct examination. She had him testify that he received $500 from Wilson. Then Beth's questioning turned to him lying to the detectives. Pablo readily admitted that earlier he wasn't honest when he was interviewed by the detectives. Beth specifically indicated why he hadn't been candid with the police. Pablo said that he didn't want to go to jail for the rest of his life. Further he didn't want to get his friend Erik Monroy involved since Erik hadn't been arrested and wasn't in jail.

Eventually he admitted that he wanted some type of deal so he could someday get out of prison. Beth felt that she could soften the blow of what was about to happen to Pablo if she would be direct and honest with the jurors. She knew that Pablo could be described as being dimwitted compared to Erik. Without a doubt Pablo was going to have great difficulty under the intense Defense cross-examination that was about to befall him. There was nothing further that Beth could do to shore up the testimony of an accomplice such as Pablo.

The direct testimony of Pablo ended as follows:

Q. WHEN YOU WENT THROUGH WHAT HAD HAPPENED. THE DETAILS OF WHAT HAD HAPPENED, IN RESPONSE TO MY QUESTIONS DID YOU TELL THE TRUTH?

A. YES

PROSECUTOR SILVERMAN: I HAVE NOTHING FURTHER AT THIS TIME.

THE COURT: CROSS

DEFENSE ATTORNEY: BEFORE YOU TESTIFIED ON FRIDAY HAVE YOU MET WITH THE PROSECUTOR AND OR THE DETECTIVES TO PREPARE YOU FOR THIS TRIAL?

A. WHAT DO YOU MEAN?

All that Beth could do was hope and pray that Pablo would be able to withstand the next couple of hours of grueling cross-examination.

CHAPTER 35- DETECTIVE KIRBY AS WITNESS

Beth knew that the cross-examination of Pablo would be brutal and she was right. The Defense attorney was able to confuse and excoriate poor Pablo who might have thought that his plea bargain wasn't such a good deal. At times during the cross-examination he might have thought life imprisonment maybe wasn't such a big deal. After Pablo's fierce cross-examination was over Beth called Detective Kirby as the prosecution's next witness. By now Beth was glad to be finished with Pablo's testimony.

Beth started with the standard questions for Detective Kirby.

Q. SIR, CAN YOU TELL US WHAT IT IS THAT YOU DO?

A. I'M A POLICE DETECTIVE FOR THE CITY OF LOS ANGELES ASSIGNED TO NORTH HOLLYWOOD DETECTIVES WORKING THE HOMICIDE UNIT.

Q. HOW MANY YEARS HAVE YOU BEEN SO EMPLOYED AS A PEACE OFFICER?

A. OVER TWELVE YEARS.

Q. OKAY, AND ARE YOU ONE OF THE INVESTIGATING OFFICERS ON THIS PARTICULAR CASE INVOLVING MARIA QUIJANO AND THE FOUR OTHER INDIVIDUALS WHO WERE INITIALLY CHARGED AND ARRESTED?

A. YES, IAM.

Q. AND DID YOU WORK WITH A PARTNER ON THIS CASE?

A. YES, DETECTIVE THOMPSON.

Q. I WANT TO DIRECT YOUR ATTENTION BACK TO THE DATE OF APRIL 10TH AT 2:10 A.M. THAT MORNING. DID YOU GO TO THE CRIME SCENE LOCATED IN SUN VALLEY AT ARCOLA AND STAGG STREET?

A. YES, I DID.

Q. AND WHAT DO YOU DO WHEN YOU WALK THROUGH A CRIME SYSTEM?

A. I NOTED CERTAIN EVIDENCE THAT WAS ALREADY—IT WAS STILL THERE. IT HAD NOT BEEN COLLECTED THERE. I OBSERVED THE VICTIM'S VEHICLE WITH THE VICTIM INSIDE, THE SHELL CASINGS, THE VEHICLE FLUID AND THE BILL OUT ON THE STREET.

Q. THE GAS BILL?

A. YES.

Beth had laid the foundation for this witness and went on to direct his attention to the conversation he had with the defendant Maria Quijano at 3:40 a.m. the night of the shooting at the house. She was asked if she had heard any gunshots or the sound of sirens from responding police units that evening. She indicated that she didn't hear any sounds after she went to sleep around 9:00 p.m.

When Detective Kirby asked about her relationship with her husband, she initially stated that they were on good terms. He testified, "She said that she was the queen of the home and that it was a good relationship, however, she suspected that he was having an affair over the past three to four years. She even mentioned there had been some talk about a divorce between the two of them."

He told the jury that since he had so many potential witnesses to talk to, he told her that they would get back with her later. Detective Kirby went on to testify that on the next day April 11, 2005, around 3:45 p.m. he and another detective stopped by to talk to Maria. Again, she was calm and composed and more than willing to provide basic information about her husband. When asked whether he had life insurance she mentioned that he had a Primerica life insurance policy for $225,000.

Beth changed the questioning to the topic of Maria's cellphone. The detective related that he asked Maria if she had a cellphone and what was the phone number. When asked what recent phone calls she made she indicated that she had talked to her son about dropping off some car keys. The detective asked for her son's phone number and she supplied it to him. The interview didn't last long and the detectives thanked her for her cooperation and said they would be back in contact with her.

Then Beth left the topic of the conversations with Maria and asked about the gas bill evidence.

Q. NOW I WANT TO DIRECT YOUR ATTENTION TO THE FOLLOWING DAY BEING APRIL 13, 2005. DID YOU DRIVE TO THE LOCATION THAT WAS LISTED ON THE GAS BILL?

A. YES, DETECTIVE HAINES AND I DROVE OUT THERE.

Q. WHAT WAS THE PURPOSE FOR THE TWO OF YOU DRIVING TO THAT LOCATION?

A. BECAUSE SALLY TALLES HAD ALSO SEEN A VAN LEAVING THE CRIME SCENE. I WANTED TO SEE IF POSSIBLY, THE VAN WOULD BE THERE AT THE ADDRESS LISTED ON THE BILL WHICH WAS FOUND.

Q. WHEN YOU DROVE OUT TO THIS LOCATION ON 47TH STREET DID YOU HAVE ANY IDEA THAT THE VAN WOULD BE THERE?

A. NO IDEA.

Q. YOU DID NOT KNOW AT THAT POINT IN TIME THAT THE VAN WAS CONNECTED TO THE GAS BILL?

A. NO

Q. EVENTUALLY, WHAT DID YOU SEE WHEN YOU GOT TO THE LOCATION ON 47TH STREET?

A. JUST EAST OF THE ADDRESS WHERE THE BILL WENT TO WAS A VAN EXACTLY HOW MISS TALLES HAD DESCRIBED TO ME.

Q. WHAT DO YOU MEAN EXACTLY?

A. WELL IT WAS A PRETTY DISTINCTIVE VAN THAT SHE SAW AND IT HAD THAT BIG WHITE COVERING OVER A WINDOW JUST LIKE SHE SAID.

At that point the prosecutor asked him if he took a photo of the van parked on the street. The detective explained that he took several photos as he sat in the detective car. He didn't want to be seen taking the photos not knowing who was around. Next, he related to the jury that he showed the photos to the eyewitness, Sally Talles. She immediately identified that van as being the same one she saw at the time of the shooting.

The detective said that this was the first solid lead that they had come up with. The detective went on to explain to the jury that his next step was to determine who was the registered owner of this van. The DMV records indicated that the owner was a Juan Garcia living at 726 West 81 Street. This didn't add up to the same location listed on the gas bill. The detective went on to say that it wasn't until April 17, 2005 that he was able to return to check out the van. He was disappointed to find that the van wasn't anywhere to be found. However, when he checked later in the day the van had returned. After that scare he said that he set a surveillance team to constantly check on the comings and goings of the van.

After having some testimony about the van, Beth returned to the questioning of Maria at another interview that took place at the North Hollywood LAPD station. Prior to that the detective had subpoenaed Maria's cellphone records.

A. I REQUESTED THE CALL RECORDS AND SUBSCRIBER INFORMATION FOR VARIOUS PHONE NUMBERS INVOLVED IN MY INVESTIGATION.

Q. WHY DID YOU DO THAT?

A. WELL, MISS QUIJANO HAD SPOKEN ABOUT A WOMAN CALLING HER WHO SHE BELIEVED WAS THE VICTIM'S GIRLFRIEND AND I WANTED TO GATHER MORE INFORMATION ABOUT THAT.

Q. DID YOU NOTICE ANYTHING THAT WAS OF SIGNIFICANCE TO YOU WHEN YOU REVIEWED THOSE CALLS?

A. THERE WAS A LARGE AMOUNT OF CALLS BETWEEN THE TIME RIGHT BEFORE THE VICTIM WAS KILLED AND SHORTLY AFTER DURING THE SAME TIME THAT MISS QUIJANO HAD TOLD ME SHE WAS ASLEEP.

Then he told the jury that was when he learned of all the calls between this defendant, Maria, and Oscar Alvarado. So, when he interviewed Maria at the police station on April 19, 2005, she was specifically asked about who was this Mr. Alvarado. The detective testified as to how the defendant, Maria, tried to explain that Mr. Alvarado's son rented a room from them and owed money. When asked how many calls were made to Mr. Alvarado, she claimed it was four calls that occurred during the evening.

The detective again asked questions about her husband. He explained to the jury that she claimed that he was a loving husband and a very loving man. He was also a loving father and would give his kids money when they needed it.

Then the detective testified that on April 19, 2005, they executed several search warrants. At the same time several people were arrested and taken into custody, including Maria Quijano, Oscar Alvarado and Wilson Sanchez. Beth asked the detective if he recovered anything from Maria Quijano. He explained that she had on her person the cellphone with the number (818) 919-2038.

After the search warrant testimony Beth made the transition into a discussion about law enforcement interviewing technique. The prosecutor knew that this could be misconstrued by certain jurors so she wanted all the jurors to have a complete understanding of what the detectives were trying to do during their interviews with Maria.

BETH

Q. DID YOU EMPLOY ANY TACTICS OR INTERVIEW STRATEGIES DURING YOUR INTERVIEW WITH THE DEFENDANT IN ORDER TO TRY AND GET HER TO SPEAK WITH YOU?

A. YES.

Q. CAN YOU EXPLAIN THAT TO US?

A. WELL, IN THE INTERVIEW, WHICH IS BASICALLY AN INTERROGATION, WE USED RUSES, WHICH ARE STATEMENTS THAT WE SAY THAT ARE NOT ACTUALLY TRUE, AND WE ALSO TRY TO USE OR GIVE THE PERSON JUSTIFICATIONS, KIND OF AN EASY WAY OUT TO ADMIT SOMETHING.

IT MAKES IT EASIER TO TELL US WHAT HAPPENED WITHOUT ACTUALLY MAKING THEM FEEL BAD ABOUT IT.

Q. SO, IN OTHER WORDS, YOU TRY TO GIVE THEM A WAY TO SOFTEN THEIR STORY AND STILL BE SOMEWHAT TRUTHFUL?

A. YES, KIND OF A WAY TO SAVE FACE.

Q. WHEN YOU WERE INTERVIEWING THE DEFENDANT DO YOU ATTEMPT TO BUILT RAPPORT WITH HER IN ORDER TO ESTABLISH SOME RELATIONSHIP?

A. YES.

Q. AND IS IT THAT YOU TRY OR ATTEMPT TO BUILD RAPPORT DURING AN INTERVIEW SUCH AS THE ONES THAT WE JUST LISTENED TO?

A. YOU WANT TO BUILD A RAPPORT WITH THE PERSON SO IT'S EASIER FOR THEM TO TALK TO YOU. THEY WILL WANT TO—THEY FEEL LIKE THEY CAN TALK TO YOU.

Q. FOR EXAMPLE, WE HEARD YOU MAKE CERTAIN STATEMENTS DURING THE INTERVIEW, WE DON'T BELIEVE YOU DID IT OR NO ONE WOULD BLAME YOU FOR DOING THIS.

ARE THOSE THE TYPE OF INTERVIEW TACTICS THAT YOU USE IN ORDER TO TRY AND BUILD RAPPORT WITH THE DEFENDANT TO MAKE IT EASIER FOR HER TO SPEAK?

A. YES.

Q. ARE THOSE NECESSARILY THINGS THAT YOU IN YOUR OWN MIND OR YOU AND YOUR PARTNER BELIEVE WHEN YOU USE THOSE TYPE OF TACTICS?

A. NOT AT ALL.

Q. ALL RIGHT. WHEN YOU TALKED ABOUT THE DEFENDANT HAVING A HARD LIFE AND THAT HER LIFE HAD BEEN DIFFICULT, AGAIN, ARE THOSE INTERVIEW TACTICS THAT YOU USED TO BUILD RAPPORT?

A. YES.

Beth knew this was a risky subject when the detectives aren't totally candid with the suspect. By playing the tape recordings of the defendant's statements it was clear that the jurors heard the detectives saying things that would sound to be sympathetic toward the defendant. Fortunately, this interview technique paid off for the detective and eventually for the prosecutor.

This defendant, Maria, was lying to the detectives from the 'get-go.' Originally her story was she didn't hear the shooting or the sirens of the emergency vehicle. Her daughter indicated that she heard everything and her mother was trying to quiet the dog. Later she had to change her story. Next the defendant's story was that she was asleep and the inference was that she wasn't using her phone. When the detectives showed her the phone records, all of a sudden, the story changed in that she was talking to a person. Then the story was that she may have talked to a Mr. Oscar Alvarado four times when in reality the phone records indicated that they talked some 28 times on that day.

If she were Pinocchio her nose would have been a foot long. The detectives purposely brought Alvarado into the interview room area so she, Maria, could see that Oscar had been arrested and was being interviewed. At that point the cat was out of the bag. How was she going to explain Alvarado? Then the detectives had made a poster-size chart showing where Mr. Alvarado's cellphone was being used on the night of the shooting. Also, her cellphone showed that it was receiving a cellphone call from Mr. Alvarado's cellphone which was near her house moments before her husband was murdered.

That was one of those 'got you moments.' The detectives could stop there and stop questioning the suspect. However, these detectives encouraged her to talk. They indicated that they could understand how she felt betrayed by her husband with his girlfriend and child. This was enough encouragement for the defendant to admit that she wanted to hurt her husband for all the hurt he had caused her.

The detectives planted the seed which the defendant instantly grasped upon. Her story changed drastically and now she admitted that she had hired Alvarado to harm her husband. This gave her the cover that she wanted only to harm him but not to kill him. Her explanation was that she did NOT intend her husband to be killed but only harmed in some way. However, if she had gone to law school, she would have learned that the person who only wants to harm a person is still guilty of Murder if that person dies as a result of that harm.

The most telling indication of how the defendant said too much was when the detectives saw her at the Van Nuys jail on May 1st.

Q. DURING THAT CONVERSATION DID YOU ASK THE DEFENDANT IF SHE WANTED TO SPEAK WITH YOU ANY FURTHER?

A. YES.

Q. AND WHAT, IF ANYTHING, DID THE DEFENDANT SAY TO YOU AT THAT POINT?

A. THAT SHE HAD ALREADY SAID TOO MUCH.

Beth wanted the jurors to hear that statement because it spoke volumes. By that time the defendant realized that all her storytelling had boxed her into a corner. Beth finished her direct examination of Detective Kirby and it was up to Maria's Defense attorney to try to dig her out of the deep hole she had dug for herself.

CHAPTER 36- OTHER PROSECUTION WITNESSES

In order to get all the relevant evidence before the jury Beth had to call numerous witnesses, some of whom had only a small amount of evidence to add to the case. If one were trying to put together a jigsaw puzzle these witnesses would be supplying only the small pieces to the puzzle. Although their testimony was short, they were necessary in order for the jury to get the whole picture of the case.

Cecilia Avila was the name on the gas bill. She testified that Wilson Sanchez was the boyfriend of her daughter Amy Avila and Wilson was living at her house. She identified a photo of a brown van as the one belonging to Wilson.

Amy Avila testified that she had been Wilson's girlfriend and that she gave him a utility bill from their house so that he could obtain a library card. As much as she didn't want to testify, Beth needed her to explain how the gas bill had gotten into the possession of Wilson Sanchez.

Juan Garcia was the stepfather of Wilson Sanchez and testified that he had loaned the old brown van to Wilson. He went on to explain that the van leaked power steering fluid and that the window on the driver's side was broken out and he had taped over it with plastic.

Frank Ramos got involved in this case by merely trying to be a good member of his family. He purchased a cellphone for Oscar Alvarado, who was his wife's uncle. He testified that the cellphone number (323) 804-7768 was the one that he had given to Alvarado in which Alvarado paid the monthly phone bills.

A T-Mobile representative testified that on April 2, 2005, four calls were made from Maria's cellphone to Alvarado's cellphone. On April 3, 2005, there were 22 calls from Maria's cellphone to Alvarado's cellphone. On April 9, 2005, from 4:20 p.m. until the next day at 12:40 a.m. Maria's cellphone made 20 calls to Alvarado's cellphone.

Beth could see from the jurors' expressions that this phone records testimony was not soaking in and some jurors seemed totally zoned out. She knew this testimony was going to be tedious if not boring but it was critical for her to show the relationship between the parties. What made things even more complicated was the fact that Maria's cellphone was with T-Mobile and Alvarado's was with Verizon which was a totally separate phone company.

Next Beth called the representative of Verizon Wireless to testify as to Alvarado's cellphone made eight calls on April 9, 2005, to April 10, 2005. She had to go over the same information with this representative just like the other company. If the jurors' looks could kill, Beth would have been dead. However, Beth wasn't deterred in asking such repetitive questions. She knew that at the time of the Argument she would make sense out of this esoteric cellphone testimony.

Yet there was one more issue with the cellphones which involved where the cellphones were located shortly before and after the shooting. The phone representative testified how the cellphone towers can indicate where the cellphone is being used. Beth used maps to illustrate the various locations of Alvarado's cellphone use by the hitmen as they drove from South-Central LA to Sun Valley and back.

Beth called Angel Aguilar (Tony Touch) as the next witness. He testified that he was with Pablo at a parking lot on 84th Street when Wilson drove up in his brown van. This witness said he heard Wilson, Erik and Pablo talking about getting a gun to do a mission to make some money. Even Wilson invited Angel to join them but when his other friend drove up, he decided to go with him and not Wilson.

Next was Willis Barnes who testified that on April 10, 2005, Wilson gave him a sealed envelope to keep safe. Wilson said there was several thousand dollars inside the envelope. During the early morning hours, he joined Wilson, Erik and Pablo in the van where they drank beer and smoked marijuana. He related to the jury that while they were all together in the van Erik said that they had killed a man on behalf of a woman who wanted her husband killed for abusing her daughter. Erik explained to him that they waited for the guy to come out and they shot him. And they got paid for the Murder.

Beth had two additional witnesses that she knew were not going to be big hits for the jury. The first was a bank representative from Washington Mutual who testified that their bank records showed that Maria had withdrawn $37, 893 from her bank accounts between September 2004 and April 2005. Another large withdrawal for $26,000 had been deposited to the account of Maria's son. Beth knew this witness wasn't going to reveal a 'smoking gun' but this testimony demonstrated that Maria had access to large amounts of money.

Then Beth called an executive from Primerica Life Insurance Company who testified that in 1993 Maria and Reynaldo had purchased a life insurance policy naming each other as primary beneficiaries in case of the death of their spouse. The face value of the policy was $225,000. On April 12, 2005, Maria contacted a claims agent to report Reynaldo's death but didn't indicate how he died.

There were a few other short cleanup witnesses but that was the bulk of the prosecution's case. Beth was glad to get to the end and announce to the court that she had no further witnesses. Then it was up to the Defense to call whatever witnesses they wanted to call on behalf of the defendant, Maria Quijano. The thrust of the Defense was to try to show that Pablo and Erik weren't reliable trustworthy witnesses. The Defense attorney had relied on the cross-examination to discredit the prosecution witnesses. The Defense case wasn't relying on additional witnesses being called but waiting for the Argument phase to attack the weaknesses in the DA's Case.

CHAPTER 37- ARGUMENT- EXPLAINING THE LAW

As soon as the last witness was finished testifying, the judge started reading instructions to the jury. This is the time when the judge explains the rules that the jurors must follow in their deliberations. For many this is considered to be the most boring time of any trial. The attorneys and court staff have heard these instructions given so many times they could verbally recite them in their sleep. The spectators in the audience can be seen yawning with some of them dozing off with their eyes closed. Yet the jurors are seated on the edge of their seats as though listening to a minister giving a damnation sermon. However, after the judge has been reading the jury instructions in a monotone voice for ten minutes, the jurors' expressions turn to a more comatose look.

When the judge is finished reading the jury instructions there is always a pregnant silence in the courtroom. No one knows whether to applaud or cheer that it is over. However, the jury instructions are the number one reasons for convictions being reversed on appeal. The Criminal Justice System has a fixation on the wording of the jury instructions. The appellate courts will analyze every word of the jury instructions and they assume that every juror will comprehend every word they hear during the jury instructions. Since the jury instructions are written in legalese, it is a stretch of logic to believe lay people who are picked as jurors really understand all the convoluted language the judge reads to them.

After the reading of the jury instructions, it is time for the attorneys to argue their cases. The prosecutor is the first to argue to the jury, then the Defense argues followed by the prosecutor who has a chance to rebut the Defense. The purpose for that procedure is that the prosecution has the burden of proof and is given a chance to answer whatever the Defense has raised. Very often the prosecutor has no idea what the Defense will be until the Defense attorney makes his or her Argument.

In this case the Defense had tipped their hand as to what the Defense was going to be. The Defense attorney had clearly implied by his questioning and statements to the jury that the defendant Maria had no intention of killing her husband. Basically, the Defense attorney wanted to blame Alvarado and the hitmen for going too far. The Defense's claim was that the defendant wasn't guilty of Murder even though the hitmen might be guilty of Murder

Beth knew she had a difficult task in that she had to educate the jurors on the law that they had to follow if they were to convict the defendant. First off, Beth needed to explain how the defendant could be guilty of Murder even though she didn't actually do the killing by pulling the trigger.

Beth decided it was more logical to start by explaining the defendant's role in the crime. Obviously, she was not the actual person who did the killing but was the person who put everything into motion. Beth needed to discuss the legal concept of who is a Principal to a crime. The law states that both the actual person who commits the crime as well as the person who aids and abets the crime are equally guilty. Beth used the below chart to show that the defendant, Maria, was a Principal.

PRINCIPALS

- A person may be guilty of a crime in two ways:
  1) She directly committed the crime, or
  2) She aided and abetted someone else ("the perpetrator") who committed the crime.
- A person is equally guilty of the crime whether she committed it personally or aided & abetted the perpetrator who committed it.

The prosecutor needed the jurors to understand that the defendant intended to aid and abet the crime that the perpetrator committed which was the killing. Beth flashed on the courtroom screen the below slide defining Aiding and Abetting.

AIDING & ABETTING INTENDED CRIMES

1. The perpetrator committed the crime,
2. The defendant knew the perpetrator was going to commit the crime,
3. Before or during the crime, the defendant intended to aid & abet the perpetrator in committing the crime, and
4. The defendant's words or conduct did in fact aid & abet the perpetrator in committing the crime.

   = To aid, facilitate, instigate, encourage or promote

Beth gave examples of the defendant's actions that showed she was aiding and abetting when she purposely sent her husband to leave the house to get something for her. Also, she talked to Wilson explaining how abusive her husband was. Later she was the one who made the decision to release the money to the hitmen after the shooting.

After Beth felt the jurors firmly understood defendant's role in the crime, she directed her attention on explaining the elements of Murder. The most important issue involved in Murder is the element of Malice which can be proven in two ways. Express Malice is the most common way it is established. But in this case the prosecutor wanted the jurors to understand Implied Malice. Beth knew the Defense would claim the defendant only intended that the victim be beaten up. The prosecution wanted to argue that beating up someone is a form of Implied Malice.

Below is the slide that Beth used when she discussed the issue of Malice.

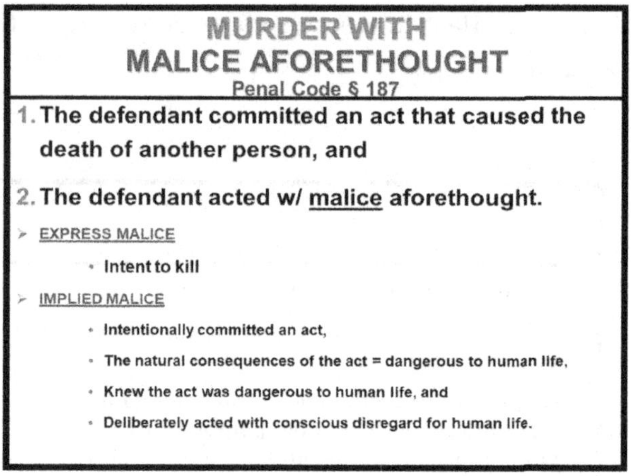

In order to prove that this Murder was a First-Degree Murder, Beth needed to review with the jurors the legal concept of Deliberation and Premeditation. This requires that the defendant must have thought and considered her actions before the crime was committed. Beth explained that the defendant had multiple discussions about the killing long before the shooting. Also, she withdrew money from her bank account months early so she could pay for the killing.

The below slide was used to discuss the issue of Deliberate and Premeditated.

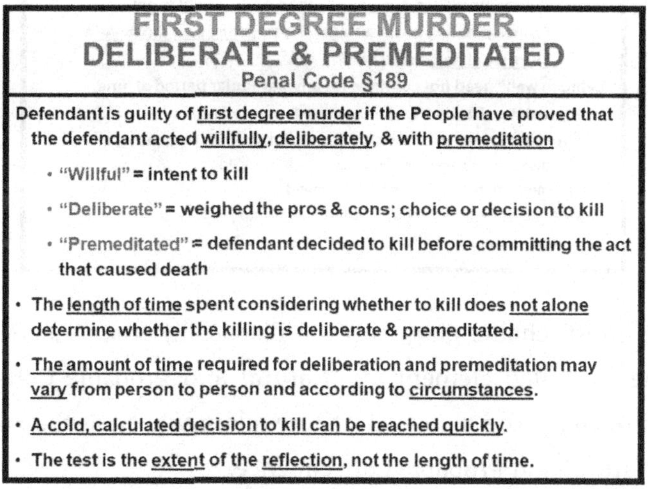

What made the prosecutor's job more difficult was that First-Degree Murder could be proven in another way. Besides the usual Premeditation and Deliberation, the law permits the prosecution to prove First Degree Murder By Lying In Wait. The problem with this legal concept in this case was that Maria didn't do the individual acts that constituted Lying in Wait. She didn't conceal herself, watch for an opportunity to act, and make a surprise attack. It was the hitmen who committed those acts that constitute the Lying in Wait. Beth needed the jurors to understand that it wasn't necessary for this defendant to actually do the acts of Lying In Wait.

FIRST DEGREE MURDER
BY LYING IN WAIT
Penal Code §189

Defendant is guilty of <u>First Degree Murder</u> if the People have proved that the defendant murdered while <u>Lying in Wait:</u>

1. Defendant <u>concealed her purpose</u> from the person killed,
2. Defendant <u>waited & watched for an opportunity</u> to act, and
3. From a position of advantage, she <u>intended to & did make a surprise attack</u> on the victim.

"Lying in wait" need not continue for any particular period of time.
It's a state of mind = to deliberation & premeditation.
"Deliberate" = weighing the pros & cons, & knowing consequences, defendant decides to act.
"Premeditation" = considered beforehand.

- *Victim can be aware of defendant's physical presence.*
- *Concealment can be by ambush or some secret plan.*

But the most challenging part of discussing the Murder elements, involved the so-called element of "Natural and Probable Consequences." The prosecutor used the below chart to explain what are the requirements to prove a Natural and Probable Consequence.

MURDER
BY NATURAL & PROBABLE CONSEQUENCES
Penal Code § 187

- **An act causes death if the death is the direct, natural, & probable consequence of the act & the death would not have happened without the act.**
- **A *<u>Natural & Probable Consequence</u>* is one that a <u>reasonable person</u> would know is <u>likely</u> to happen if nothing unusual intervenes. In deciding whether a consequence is natural & probable, consider <u>all</u> of the circumstances established by the evidence.**

In order to make sure that the jury understood that the Natural and Probable Consequence of her action, the prosecutor superimposed the facts that proved up this legal concept.

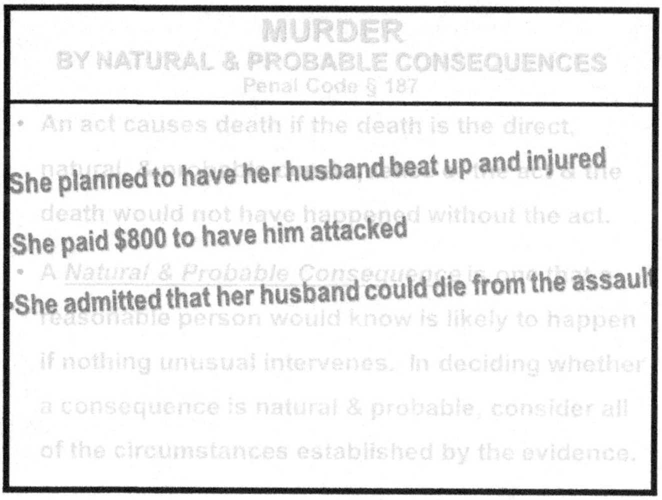

This instruction on Natural and Probable Consequences applied only if the jury believed the defendant's story that she intended to merely harm her husband. The theory of this legal concept is that society believes that criminals should be accountable for their criminal conduct which foreseeably can result in death. In this situation a reasonable person would know that it was foreseeable that a victim could die from a beating even if the defendant didn't actually intend the victim to die.

CHAPTER 38- ARGUMENT- EXPLAINING THE LAW OF CONSPIRACY

There was no question that this Murder case involved a conspiracy between several people. There was the person (Maria the wife) who hired and paid to have someone killed; there was the middleman (Oscar Alvarado) who put the plan in motion; and ultimately there were the hitmen which consisted of the triggerman (Wilson Sanchez), the getaway driver (Erik Monroy), and the lookout (Pablo Alvarenga).

But the prosecutor has to make a strategic decision whether to charge all the defendants with the basic charge of Murder or charge them all with the crime of Conspiracy to Commit Murder. Many prosecutors will not charge the suspects with the crime of Conspiracy to Commit Murder because the law is so complex and difficult for jurors to understand. Those prosecutors believe that there is always the possibility that the jurors will become so confused that they will not be able to reach a verdict against all the parties.

CONSPIRACY TO COMMIT MURDER
Penal Code § 182

1. **The defendant intended to agree & did agree with another to intentionally kill,**
2. **At the time of the agreement, defendant & another co-conspirator intended that 1 or more of the co-conspirators would intentionally kill,**
3. **Def or 1 of the members of the conspiracy committed at least 1 overt act to accomplish the murder, and**
4. **At least 1 of the overt acts was committed in California.**

The above chart tries to explain to the jurors the legal concept of Conspiracy to Commit Murder. This requires that at least two parties have to agree to kill someone. Some jurors can become confused believing that there has to be a formal agreement to do a killing. Other jurors might think all the parties have to be present at the time of the agreement.

Then there is the requirement that the defendant and a co-conspirator have to intend that one of the co-conspirators actually do the killing of the victim. Further, there is the requirement that the jury must find that one of the overt acts was committed in California. Jurors can become so confused as to what is an overt act and how are they proved to the jurors?

In other words, trying to prove the charge of Conspiracy to Commit Murder is not an easy task. There are so many places that the jurors can become lost and can't figure out what they are to do or find. However, in this case with so many co-conspirators, Beth decided it was essential to charge and prove the crime of Conspiracy to Commit Murder. She used the below chart to explain each of the complicated points of a conspiracy.

CONSPIRACY TO COMMIT MURDER
Penal Code § 182

- **The People *do not* have to prove all the conspirators:**
  - **Actually met or know another**
  - **Came to a formal agreement**
- **An "overt act" is:**
  - **An act by 1 or more of the conspirators done to help accomplish the murder.**
  - **An overt act does not have to be a criminal act itself.**
- **All co-conspirators held equally responsible for all acts done by any of the group of conspirators in furtherance of the conspiracy.**

Beth spent considerable time explaining that not all the co-conspirators had to meet together to hatch the plan to Murder the victim. There was testimony from the hitmen that they had never met Maria before the time they were driving to the Valley to kill her husband. The prosecutor stressed that an overt act only had to be done by one of the co-conspirators. Beth told the jurors that if they had found just one of the overt acts had been proven to their satisfaction, they didn't need to go on to consider all the other overt acts. She was trying to make sure that the jurors didn't waste their time and become bogged done trying to determine if every overt act had been proven.

In order to make it perfectly clear to the jurors who were the Parties to the Conspiracy she used the below slide in her Argument. She explained that the big circle was the Conspiracy and everyone who was inside the circle was a co-conspirator. At the top was the hirer who in this case was the defendant, Maria, and in the center was the middleman Alvarado. At the bottom were the hitmen with Wilson Sanchez directly below Alvarado the middlemen. To the left side of Wilson were the driver Erik and lookout Pablo who were part of the Conspiracy but had a lesser role in the killing.

Next to Wilson Sanchez, Beth used a clip art of a gun to illustrate he was the shooter. The red arrow represented the bullets which were fired at the victim, Reynaldo, who was depicted outside the circle of the conspiracy. The prosecutor used this slide numerous times during her Argument. It was like an anchor which the jurors could use to put the parties in perspective as to their roles they played in the shooting.

Beth being a veteran prosecutor understood that she couldn't risk having jurors becoming confounded with the 22 Overt Acts of the Conspiracy. Below was the slide summarizing the first five overt acts.

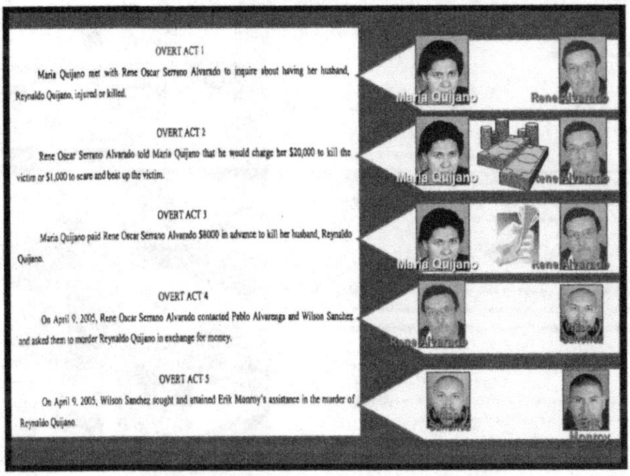

That slide was followed by another one showing six more overt acts.

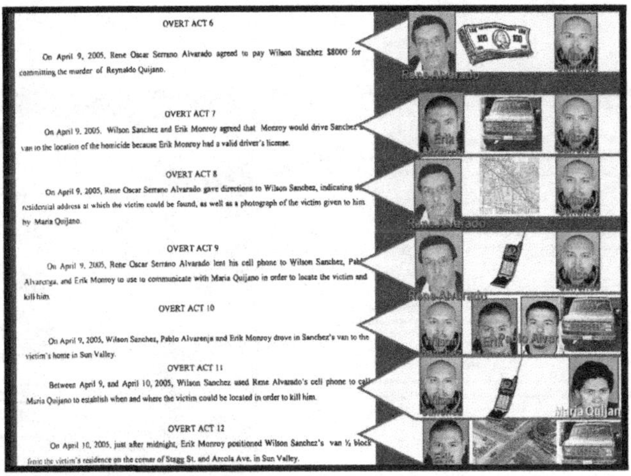

The next slide was similar.

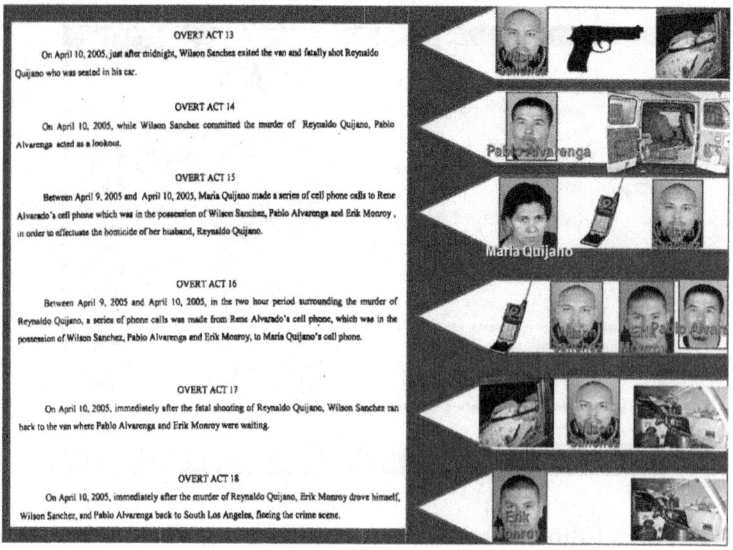

This was the last slide illustrating the remaining overt acts.

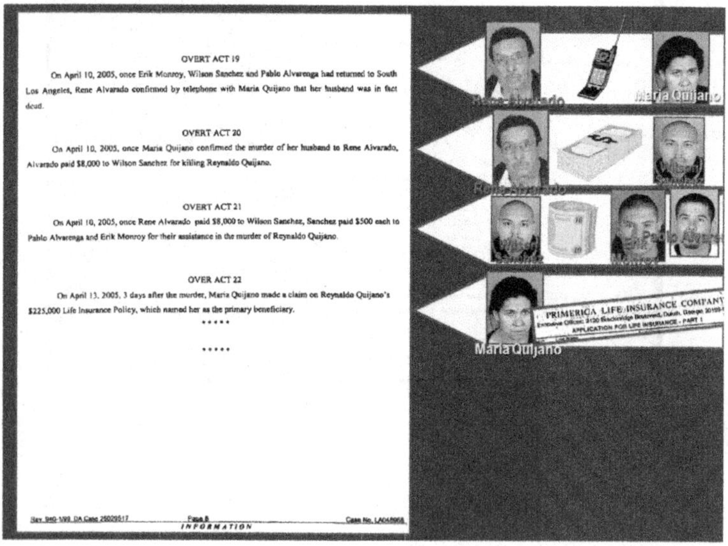

After this last slide the jurors were sufficiently introduced to the law and facts as to Overt Acts. Beth continually stressed in her Argument that they as jurors had to find at least one overt act had been committed. Her hope was that the jurors not get bogged down on deciding each and every overt act.

CHAPTER 39 ARGUMENT- EXPLAINING PHONE RECORDS

At this point in Beth's Argument, she had to move on to another perplexing factual topic which involved the phone records. She couldn't afford to lose any of the jurors regarding the meaning and significance of the cellphone evidence. She decided to start with Alvarado's cellphone. What made it unclear was the fact that Alvarado's cellphone was not registered in his name. Because of Alvarado's checkered financial past, he couldn't obtain a cellphone in his own name. That was when he asked a relative to obtain a cellphone for him and Alvarado agreed to pay the cellphone bill every month.

In order for none of the jurors to become lost, Beth used the below slide showing that the cellphone (323) 804-7768 was registered to a Franck Ramos (pseudonym). On this slide Beth showed how this witness Mr. Ramos testified to purchasing the cellphone and giving it to Alvarado to be used under the name Rene Serrano which was a name used by Alvarado. Beth listed on this slide all the evidence that the jury had heard about Alvarado using and possessing this phone.

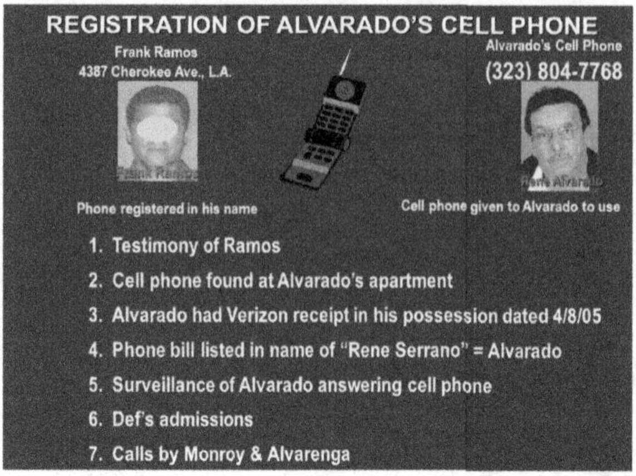

Once the prosecutor was confident that the jury grasped that the number (323) 804-7768 was co-conspirator Alvarado's cellphone number, then Beth wanted the jury to remember how many phone calls were made to Alvarado from this defendant, Maria. During the trial the prosecution called phone company representative who testified to reviewing the phone records of the phones (818) 919-2038 (Maria's cellphone) and (323) 8047768 (Alvarado's cellphone).

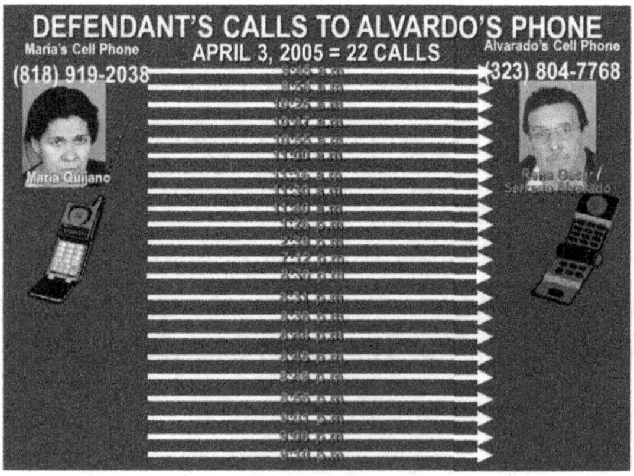

Beth used two slides, one showing all the calls by Maria to Alvarado between the two on April 3, 2005, (totaling 22 calls) and another slide showing the calls made on April 9 and 10 (totaling 24 calls).

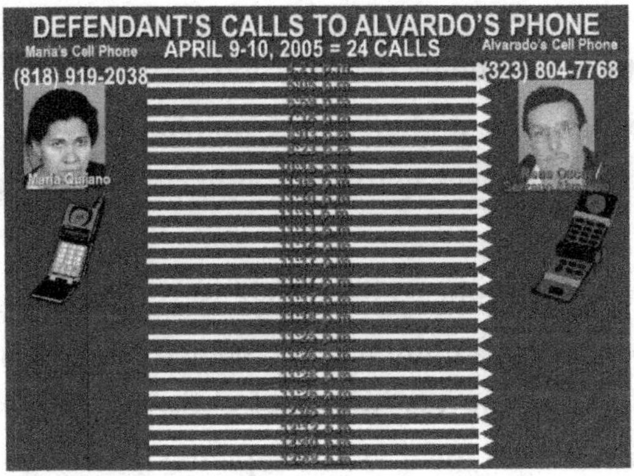

Next the prosecutor wanted to convey to the jurors how many calls Alvarado made to the defendant. This below slide shows that there were eight phone calls from Alvarado to defendant Maria between April 9th and 10th.

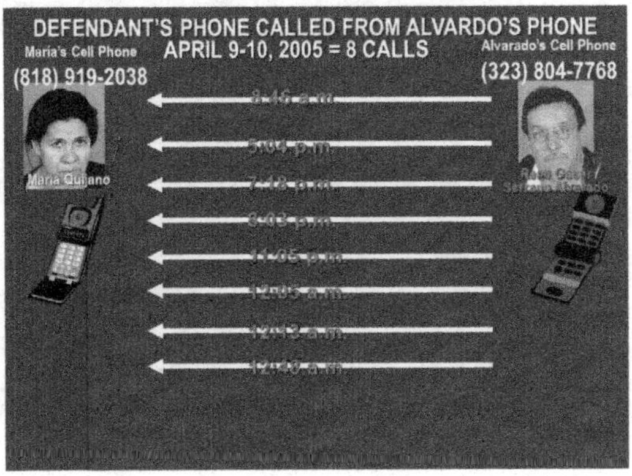

Using the above slides was the best way to show that the phone records helped to prove the contact between members of the conspiracy. A slide/chart showing the number of phone calls between the two was a better method to convey the voluminous cellphone records. Merely giving the jurors a stack of phone records and expecting them to review the massive number of pages and glean the number of phone calls between the parties wasn't an effective way to communicate all that data.

There were other phone calls which were relevant in this case. The prosecution was relying on phone calls made by co-conspirators to provide the corroboration for the testimony of Erik and Pablo. The below slide showed that Wilson used Alvarado's cellphone to call the defendant, Maria. Erik used that cellphone to call his mother and he was interrupted when Maria called that cellphone. Since Erik was a co-conspirator, his testimony needed to be corroborated by independent facts. The below slide was used to show that Erik did in fact use that cellphone when Maria made contact.

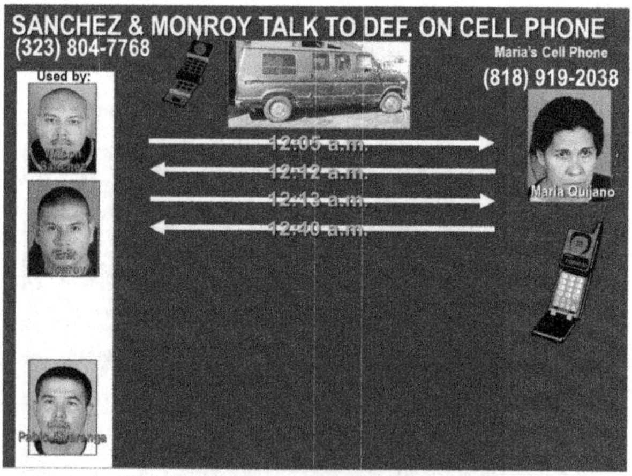

Beth used an additional slide seen below which showed that Erik made phone calls to his mother and girlfriend who testified that they received such calls from Erik.

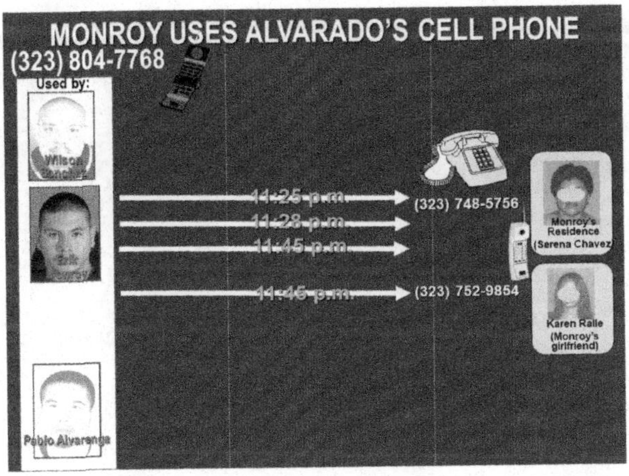

CHAPTER 40-ARGUMENT-CELLPHONE TOWERS

After Beth had finished discussing the phone records, she had another task of explaining where the cellphone calls were made and where they were received. For years law enforcement wasn't able to show where the suspects were located when making or receiving phone calls. However, today cellphone calls can be tracked by the cellphone towers which are activated by those calls. True it can't show precisely where a suspect or witness is located but it can show the immediate vicinity where the calls were made or received (approximately within a half a block or 1500 feet).

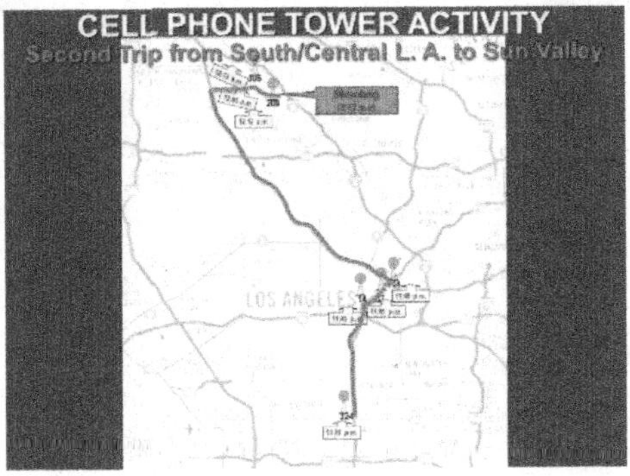

Beth used the below slide to illustrate the cell towers that were activated when the hitmen were using Alvarado's cellphone while traveling to and from the crime scene. The cell towers that were activated were precisely along the freeway route used by the hitmen to travel to the Valley in Wilson's van. The location of the cell towers provided the corroboration to support the testimony of Erik and Pablo as to the route they traveled to the location of the crime scene.

The below slide is similar to the other one, but this time it shows the return route traveled by the hitmen from the crime scene to their homes in South-Central Los Angeles.

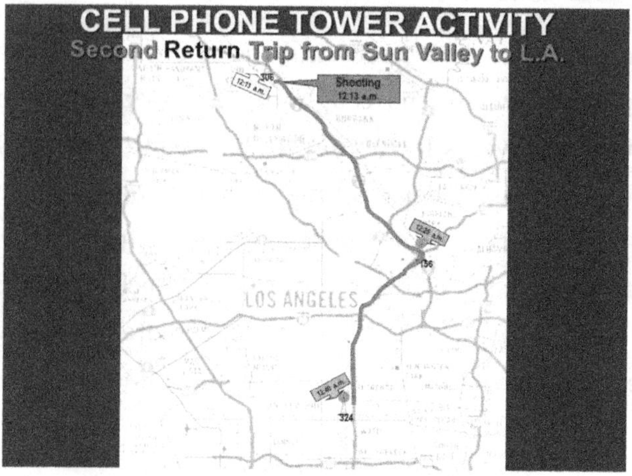

In order to assure that the jurors understood that the hitmen used different routes of travel going to and returning to the shooting, Beth used this slide which combined the freeway travel to and from the shooting scene.

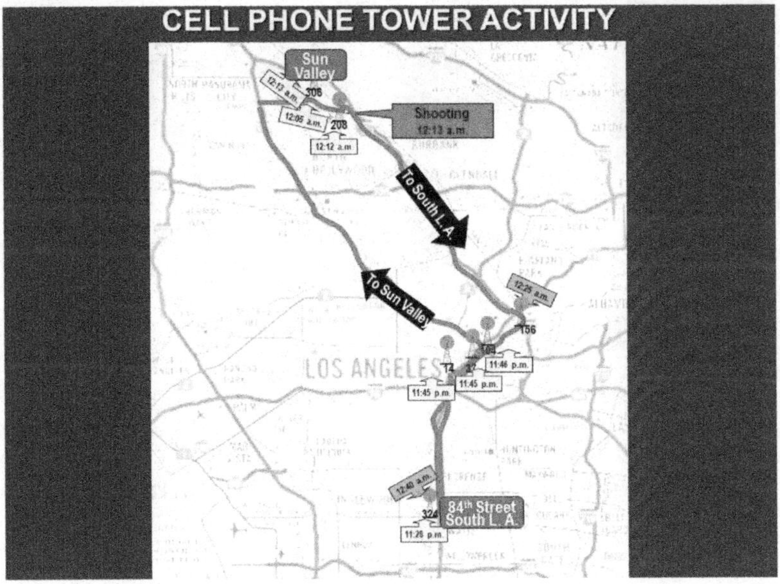

CHAPTER 41- ARGUMENT- MOTIVE, INSURANCE, & BANK RECORDS

The prosecution is not required to prove that the defendant had a motive to kill the victim. The law recognizes that in many Murders, the defendant doesn't even know or ever had contact with the victim. Therefore, motive is not required to be proven by the prosecution but if it does exist, it can be used to prove that the defendant committed the crime. In this case Beth wanted to show that there were a number of facts that showed that Maria had a motive to kill her husband.

The below slide/chart was used by the prosecution to show the jury the law regarding Motive.

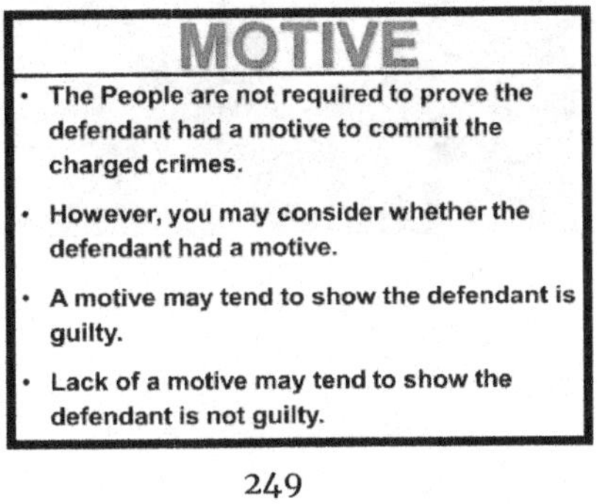

Beth used the below slide to illustrate how the defendant was angry with her husband having an affair and a child with another woman. Even though the defendant claimed that the victim molested her daughter which may or may not have been true but Beth listed it with question marks.

In Beth's slide show she used the below slide to illustrate who was involved and the connection between each person in what could be described as a lover's triangle.

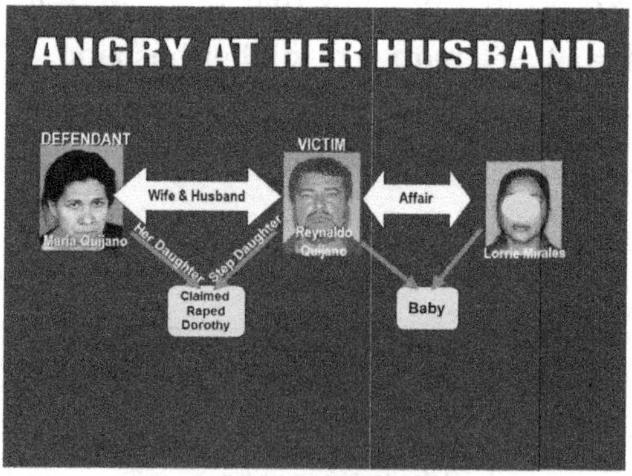

Next Beth wanted the jurors to consider the fact that the defendant would gain considerable money upon her husband's death. Beth showed that the defendant didn't waste any time putting in a life insurance claim as beneficiary to her husband's policy for $225,000.

In order for the jury to have no doubt about the Life Insurance claim, Beth used the below slide showing the actual Primerica Life Insurance Company policy with the defendant's photo inserted.

This showed that the defendant not only had ‘murder on her mind’ but also ‘money on her mind.’

CHAPTER 42- ARGUMENT- DEFENDANT LYING TO THE POLICE

One of the most difficult legal issues for prosecutors to convey to jurors is what is called Consciousness of Guilt. This can occur when a defendant makes false statements to detectives about the crime knowing them to be false. This deception may be considered in determining the guilt of that individual.

The below chart was used by the prosecution to explain Consciousness of Guilt to the jurors.

CONSCIOUSNESS OF GUILT – FALSE STATEMENTS

- **If the defendant made a false or misleading statement relating to the crime, knowing it was false or intending to mislead, that conduct may show she was aware of her guilt of the crime, and may be considered in determining her guilt.**
- **It is up to you to decide its meaning and importance. Such a statement cannot prove guilt by itself.**

In order to use Consciousness of Guilt to convict this defendant, Beth needed to go through each of Maria's statements that were false. Next Beth needed to show that Maria knew that her statement was false and that the deception was done to mislead the detectives.

Beth decided to approach the pattern of lying in a chronological order. She started with the initial statement the defendant gave to the detectives only a short time after the killing. That was when she was feigning a total lack of knowledge of what was going on. Beth used the below slide to show what the defendant initially said.

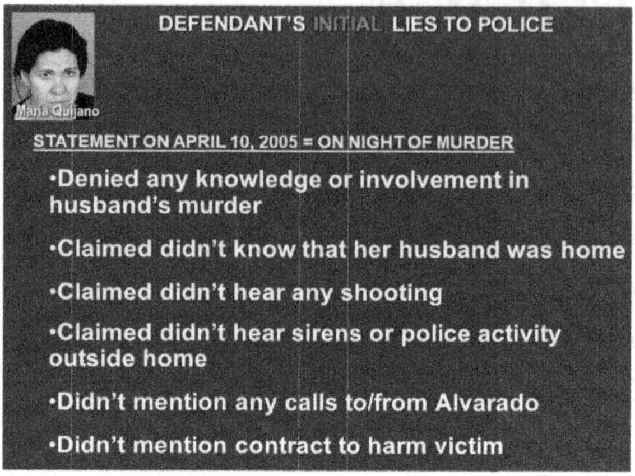

The next thing the prosecutor did was interpose the words 'Are Her Statements REASONABLE?' on top of this initial statement. In this way the jurors could see for themselves how the defendant was lying.

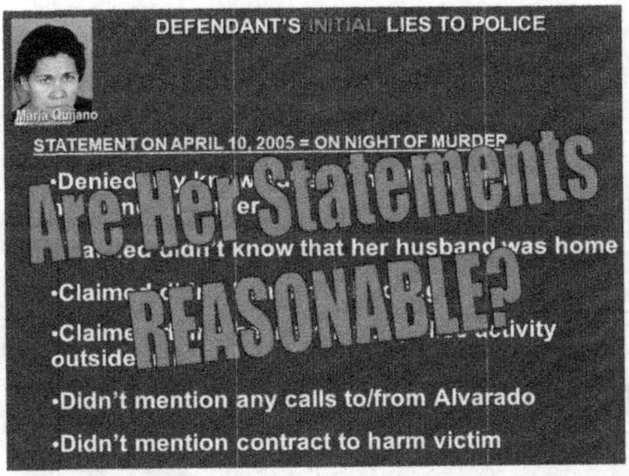

On the day following the shooting, the detectives had another conversation with the defendant. This time she added information about a life insurance policy. However, this time, she mentioned that her husband had come home from work after 9:00 p.m. Still there was no mention of being in contact with Oscar Alvarado.

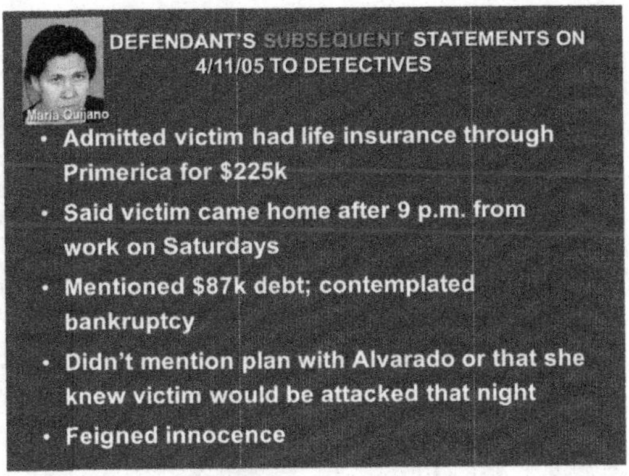

About a week after the shooting the detectives had another conversation with the defendant. This time she made an outlandish statement about her husband's father.

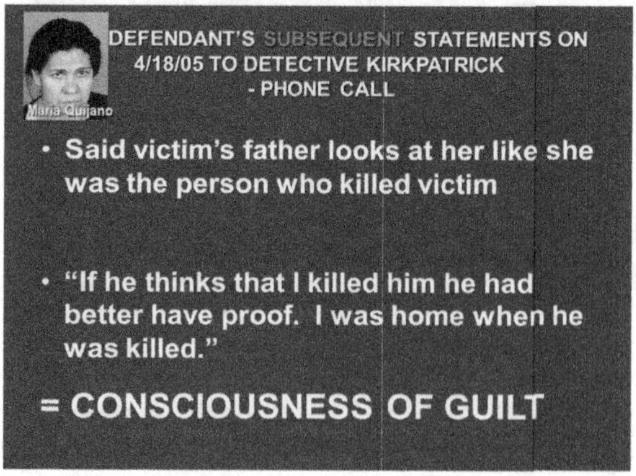

It wasn't until April 19th that the detectives were back in contact with the defendant and she wasn't truthful about the life insurance policy. Also, she didn't mention dealing with Alvarado or the fact that she only wanted her husband beat up.

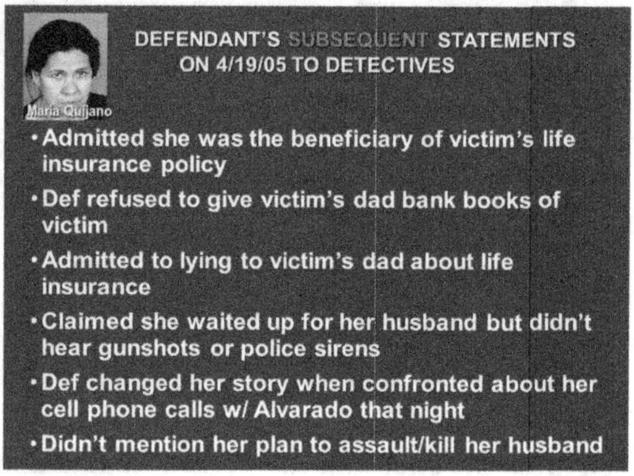

Additionally, on April 19th she told the detectives that Alvarado didn't come over that night. Also, she gave a statement that she and her husband had a great relationship but she added that his Murder was result of his mistakes with his girlfriend.

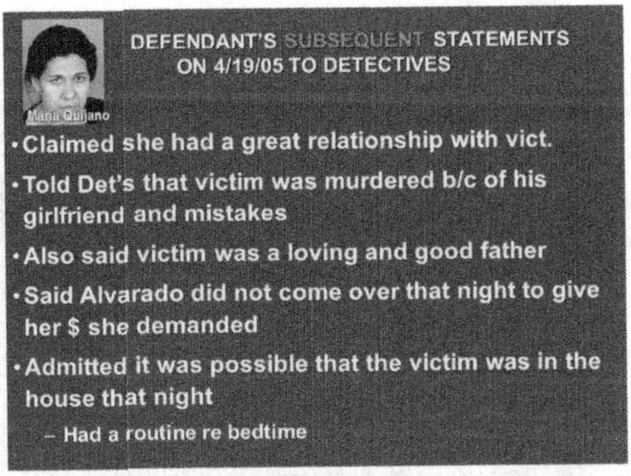

Finally on April 28, 2005, she was arrested and had a epiphany spiritual moment. She wanted and needed to convince the detective that she didn't do anything wrong. This time she admitted to being angry with her husband for his infidelity. There was a willingness to say that she had talked to Alvarado a few times.

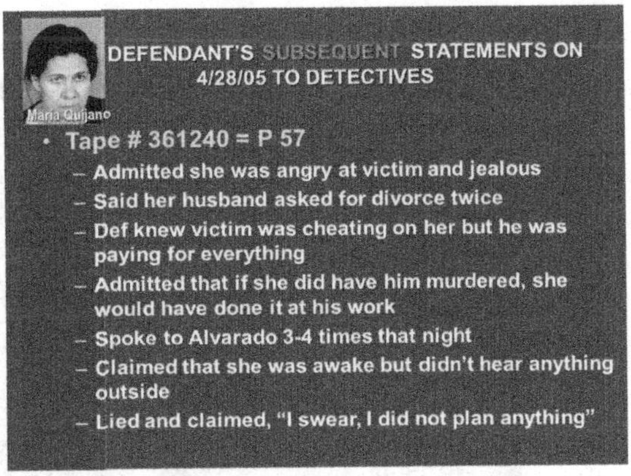

She continued to talk to the detective and tried to appear to be the victim. For the first time she suggested that things might have gotten out of hand. She stressed that she didn't plan to do anything wrong to the victim.

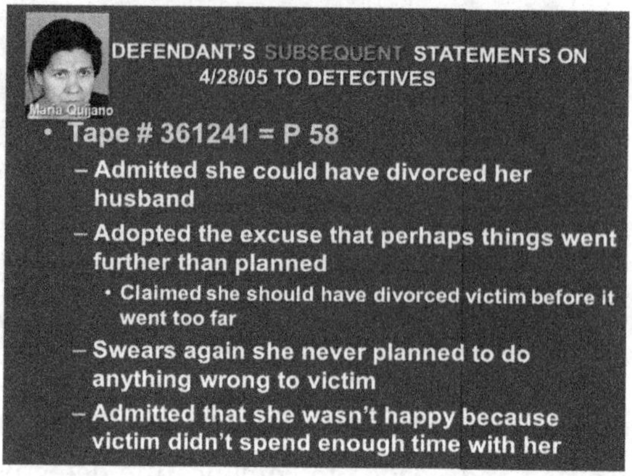

She continued to talk to the detective on April 28th when she was arrested. Now she was willing to admit that she had talked to Alvarado around 10:30 p.m. and that now she claimed she was a light sleeper.

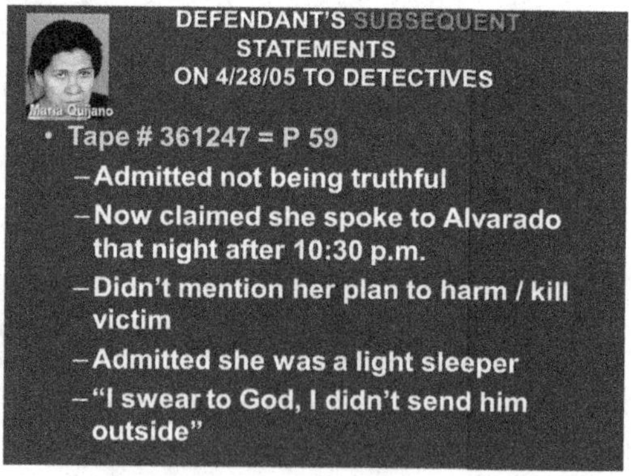

The next day April 29, 2005, Edward Younger interviewed her separately. In this conversation she admitted planning with Alvarado to do bad things to her husband.

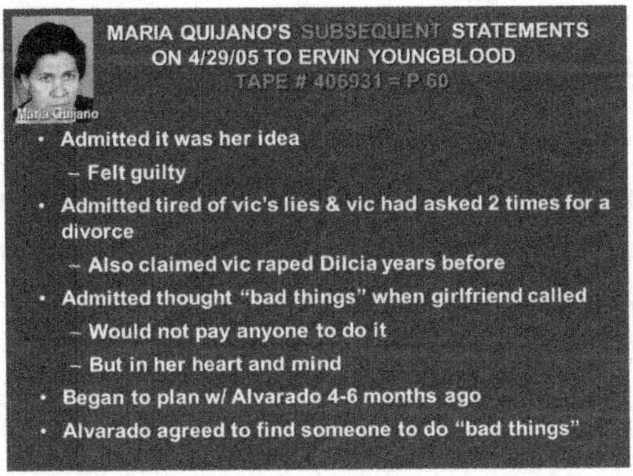

During this interview with Edward Younger, the defendant revealed the discussion about the possibility of killing her husband.

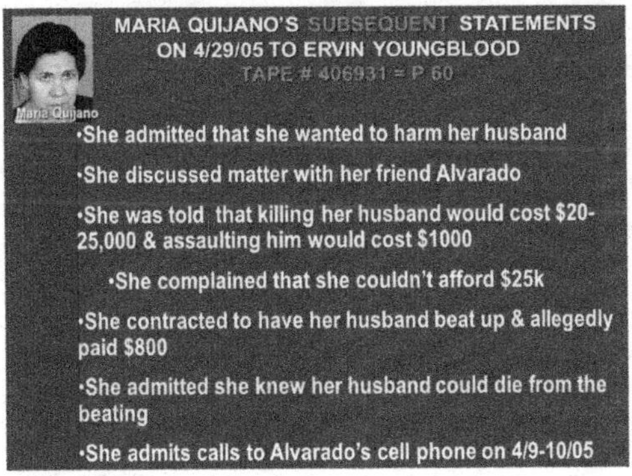

Finally, at the end of Edward Younger's interview with defendant she was willing to concede that she planned to have her husband beat up for $800. She claimed she couldn't afford the $25,000 to have him killed. But she was aware that he could die from the beating.

Discussing the legal concept of consciousness of guilt was a tedious process. But Beth thought it was necessary to prove the fact that she was continuously lying every time she talked to the detectives. Beth argued that the defendant's conduct was proof of a Consciousness of Guilt.

In addition to using all of these various statements Beth was able to use them as a partial admission. Although the defendant didn't confess to setting up the Murder of her husband, she was willing to say that she did set up a beating of her husband that could result in his death. Beth wanted the jurors to see how these statements helped to prove the Natural and Probable Consequences of Murder.

CHAPTER 43- SUMMARIZING THE EVIDENCE, DEFENSE ARGUMENT AND REBUTTAL

Beth had been arguing for over an hour and she could see that the lengthy discussion on the Consciousness of Guilt was wearing down the jurors' attention span. She had calculated that her Argument would be lengthy because she wanted to cover all the legal issues. She didn't want to take a chance that a rogue juror would somehow think that if something wasn't covered by the prosecutor that it was a weakness in the DA's case therefore creating REASONABLE DOUBT.

She had one last slide in her slide show which she wanted to use to summarize the evidence. It is called the EVIDENCE POINTING TO THE DEFENDANT'S GUILT. She methodically listed the various pieces of evidence in each arrow which pointed to the defendant. This method of arguing allows the jurors to see the cumulative effect of the evidence. This is an effective way to summarize all the prosecution evidence.

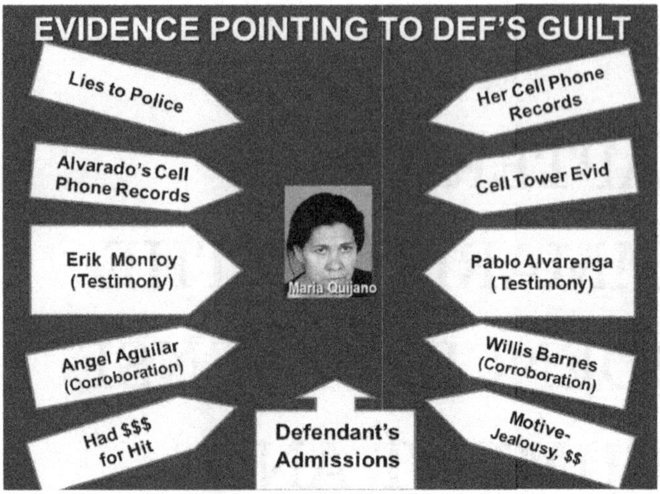

Beth finished with the last point being the so-called 'Defendant's Admissions.' Beth wanted to close strong so she told the jurors to look at all the evidence that proved the prosecution's case. As Beth gently picked up her papers from the lectern she glanced up at the jurors. Then with a grim look on her face and a fervent voice laced with sincerity, she said, "This defendant is guilty of Murder and Conspiracy to Commit Murder." Her words seemed to reverberate off the oak-paneled walls of the courtroom. No one said a word as she turned to walk over to the counsel table. Just before she reached her seat, she turned slightly back to face the jurors and softly utter, "Thank you for your attention." Then she sat down in the DA's chair.

After she was seated, the Defense attorney gathered up his notes and slowly walked over to the lectern. As Beth had predicted he immediately attacked the most vulnerable part of the DA's case. He zeroed in on the testimony of Erik Monroy and Pablo Alvarenga who he claimed were admitted liars. The Defense attorney continued hammering away at the plea bargain which both co-conspirators received from the DA's Office. He tried to imply that both witnesses Erik and Pablo were motivated to lie in order to get a sentence of only 22 years in prison for Manslaughter charge instead of a life sentence on a Murder conviction.

Beth couldn't help noticing that some of the jurors seemed to be engrossed in the Defense attorney's contention. Then the Defense attorney changed his attack on the prosecution's case by claiming that the other co-conspirators were the ones at fault. He claimed that Maria only intended to harm her husband but not wanting him killed. He tried to create sympathy for Maria and scorn for her 'two-timing' husband who had a mistress and a newborn by that woman. Undoubtedly some of the women jurors had to feel some compassion for Maria. She did give the appearance of a betrayed woman who didn't know how to get out of the doldrums she found herself in.

The Defense Argument was that Maria wanted only for her husband to feel some degree of pain for the hurt he had caused her. The real culprits were the hitmen who went too far. She shouldn't be held responsible for some action of those overzealous goons. Then the Defense attorney went into the usual claim that the prosecution hadn't proved their case beyond a reasonable doubt. There was no eyewitness to prove she did the shooting. No one testified that she specifically paid anyone money to kill her husband.

The Defense stressed that Maria never admitted to the detectives that she wanted her husband killed. The Defense attorney continued to tell the jury all the times she made statements to only harm her husband. Never did she admit every hiring anyone to kill her husband. The entire Defense Argument had some compelling elements and gave the jurors food for thought.

After the Defense attorney had finished it was time for the prosecutor to rebut the Defense's claims. Beth picked up her notes that she had written during the Defense Argument. She slowly and deliberately carried those papers over to the lectern. She positioned herself where she could directly see every juror's face. With a subdued voice she wanted to project to the jurors the solemn task they were about to embark on.

She indicated that the job of being a juror comes with an awesome responsibility. As jurors they have to make decisions as to what the facts were that existed sometime in the past. Then they needed to apply the law to those facts they found to be true. Beth used the below chart to illustrate for the jurors what they could and could not consider in determining the facts.

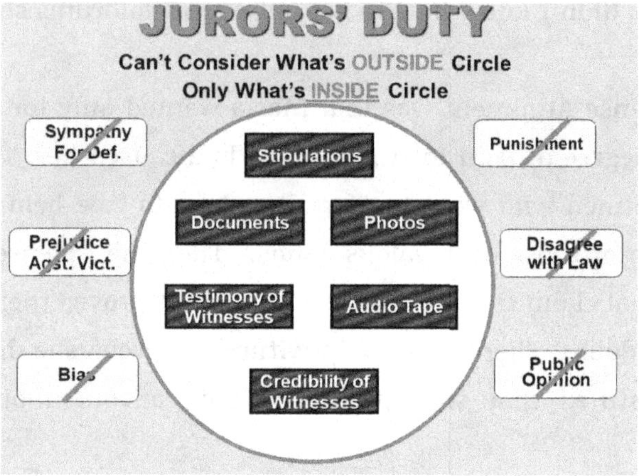

She listed inside the circle the items the jurors could consider such as witness testimony, documents, photos and tape recordings introduced into evidence, as well as evidence of credibility of witnesses plus any stipulations both parties had agreed to.

The main reason Beth used this chart was to bring to the jurors' attention that they could NOT consider sympathy for the defendant or what punishment she might receive if convicted. Beth wanted to remind the jurors that those were improper considerations. Beth recognized that there are always jurors who will feel sorry for the defendant. These jurors may possess what is called the 'undog mentality.' She knew that she needed to address those jurors' concerns.

After Beth was certain the jurors would follow the LAW, she moved on to address the Argument that Maria's attorney had made to the jury. Before the trial, Beth had talked to me, the author, about what would be an effective way to respond to the Defense's Argument. I asked her what she thought the various points that the Defense would bring up during its Argument.

I suggested that she should use the below chart which would give her a graphic way of showing where each piece of the Defense Argument belonged. She used it to evaluate each point made by the Defense attorney.

The first claim by the Defense was that the jurors should disregard both Erik and Pablo's testimony because they both had character flaws. Then Beth inserted in her Argument an old saying which was 'Crimes conceived in hell don't have angels as witnesses.' She went on to say that when you are looking for someone to do a killing for you, you will look for someone who has a jaded past. Then Beth went over to the chart and pretended to throw the bad dude argument into the Trash Can.

Then Beth shifted to the Defense Argument that this defendant didn't aid and abet the killing. She pointed out that she was the one who did all the acts to set everything in motion. She even said that she knew that the Natural and Probable consequences of this beating could result in her husband's death.

Lastly Beth wanted to address the Defense argument that the prosecution hadn't proved their case beyond a Reasonable Doubt. For that, Beth switched to the below charts titled DEFENSE MISSING THE TARGET. This gave the prosecutor a chance to discuss each of the Defense points and indicate whether they constituted Reasonable Doubt or something much less.

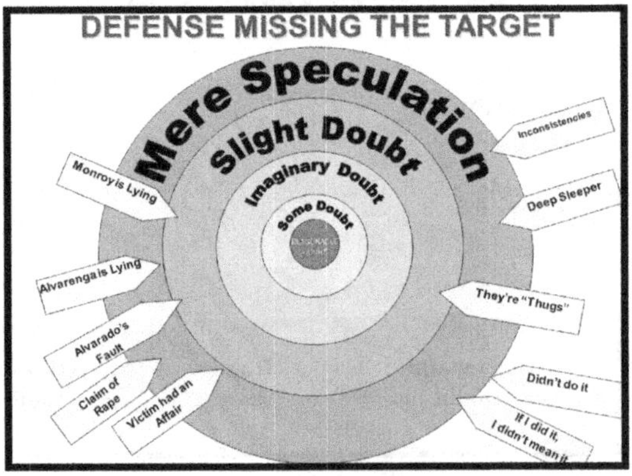

Beth used arrows to highlight each of the Defense's points and discussed what type of DOUBT each point may have created. Some of the points were no more than 'Mere Speculation.' However, Beth admitted that several points did create a slight doubt but at no time did they constitute a Reasonable Doubt. This chart seemed to help some of the jurors recognize where the various points raised by the Defense should be placed.

By this point in the Argument, Beth understood that no more time in arguing was going to change the minds of the jurors. She flashed on the screen as seen below what she wanted the jurors to remember. Then she somberly stated that the evidence proved that this defendant was GUILTY of MURDER FOR PERSONAL GAIN and GUILTY of CONSPIRACY TO MURDER.

After that Beth collected her notes from the lectern and resumed her seat at counsel table.

CHAPTER 44- VERDICT, OTHER TRIALS, & APPEALS

After the Argument was over the judge read the final jury instructions that the jury needed to abide by. The judge explained that there were a number of verdict forms that the foreperson was required to fill out properly or else the case could end in a mistrial. After that, the judge instructed the jurors to retire to the jury deliberation room.

The bailiff opened the door to the hallway leading to the deliberation room. As Beth was straightening up the papers and placing everything in her case folder, she glanced over to the jury box and saw the jurors filing out of the courtroom. Most of them had a stern look on their faces with their eyes focused directly down on the floor. Beth had to wonder what are they thinking? Are they confused or are they uncertain whether they can convict poor little Maria who sat there in court projecting the image of a frightened soul? Anyone who was seeing her for the first time couldn't help but be sympathetic to her plight.

Beth was hoping that none of the jurors had sympathy for the defendant after hearing the prosecution Argument. Beth had tried many Murder cases where the Premeditation and Deliberation was formed over a short period of time. But Maria had formed her Premeditation and Deliberation to commit Murder months earlier when she was shopping around for someone to kill her husband. She even withdrew money back in January in order to have money to pay a hitman.

When Beth had everything packed up, she stood up to leave. As she slowly turned to walk out of the courtroom she looked to the side and saw the defendant being led out of the courtroom to the custody holding cell. All of sudden Beth snapped back to reality. There was nothing more that she could do at this time. She had thoroughly prepared and presented the facts to the jurors. She had spent hours crafting her Argument to be sure she covered every issue that any juror might have.

Beth continued to walk through the courtroom to the low swinging doors leading to the spectator area. With her hands full she used her knee to push open the short swivel doors. That was when it dawned on her that it was over and it was in the hands of the jurors. As she continued to walk toward the courtroom exit doors, she heard the authoritative voice of the courtroom clerk. "Beth are you going to be in your office or in another courtroom?"

Beth stopped and looked toward the courtroom clerk and told her to use her cellphone number if any questions came up or if the jury reached a verdict. Then she scurried through the crowded ninth-floor hallway of the Criminal Courts Building. As she reached the bank of elevators, she found one going UP and got on. Within minutes she was back in her office and plunked down the case file of Maria Quijano on the corner of her desk. As though she were in a robotic mode, she reached for the file on the Oscar Rene Alvarado case. She flipped open the file and glanced at her list of things that needed to be done before trial. Without any fanfare she grabbed the phone and started making calls to the witnesses.

Back on the ninth floor of the Criminal Courts Building the jurors did their job selecting a foreperson and started their deliberations. It is next to impossible to anticipate how long it will take a jury to reach a verdict. In this case of Maria Quijano, the jurors worked their way through the evidence and exhibits and came to a unanimous verdict. Within short order the jurors returned to the courtroom and rendered a verdict of guilty against her for count 1, conspiracy to commit first-degree Murder and count 2, first-degree Murder. The jury found true the allegation as to both counts that she and her co-conspirators committed the Murder for financial gain and she was found to be a principal armed with a firearm.

Several weeks later, the judge imposed sentence which consisted of life without the possibility of parole on count 2, plus one year for the firearm enhancement. The sentence of 25 years to life plus one year for the firearm enhancement on count 1 was imposed and stayed. From that point, Maria Quijano was transported to state prison for the rest of her life.

Maria Quijano Appeal

Later she appealed her conviction and the appellate court reviewed her trial to see if there were any errors committed during the trial or in the sentencing. Her contentions on appeal were as follows:

1. The trial court erred by failing to instruct the jury that it could convict her of the target offense of aggravated assault if it had a reasonable doubt concerning her intent to have Reynaldo killed;

2. The trial court erred in erroneously instructing that a person who aids and abets is "equally guilty' of the crime committed by a perpetrator;

3. The trial court erred by giving a modified financial gain special circumstance instruction; and

4. The trial court failed to fully instruct the jury concerning its authority to convict Quijano of the lesser included offense of second-degree Murder.

After extensive briefing of the points and authority on the above issues the appellate court unanimously affirmed Maria's conviction on all the counts.

(Those readers who have developed a certain amount of sympathy for unfortunate Maria might want to consider some of her activities while awaiting trial. She had indicated that she wanted her son to be arrested so he would be sent to county jail so he could kill Oscar Alvarado. Apparently, she felt that Oscar's statements might be used against her so she wanted him dead. Further, Maria had tried to find someone who could harm the two detectives working on her case. If that wasn't enough, she wanted someone to do 'something bad' to both the original judge and the original prosecutor. Fortunately, she wasn't able to carry out any of these threats against others.)

Oscar Alvarado Trial

Shortly after Maria's conviction, Beth started the trial for Oscar Alvarado in the same judge's courtroom. The trial was very similar to Maria's except it didn't go into all of Maria's inconsistent statements since they weren't relevant to Alvarado's guilt. Beth basically called the same witnesses and they testified the same as before.

However, the main differences between the two trials was that Oscar Alvarado took the witness stand and told a unique story in hopes that some juror would believe it. Alvarado denied that Maria asked him to find someone to kill her husband or that he hired Wilson to kill Reynaldo. Further he testified that Maria gave him $8,000 to hold for her. He claimed that he met Wilson one day while he was talking on the phone with Maria.

Maria asked him to put Wilson on the cellphone. Wilson returned the cellphone to Alvarado after speaking to Maria. Wilson then asked to see the $8,000 which Alvarado showed him. Alvarado denied giving Wilson a photograph of Reynaldo. He admitted giving Wilson directions to Maria's house. Later, he gave $8,000 to Wilson at Maria's request. He testified that his previous statements were made-up stories to the police. He only told the police what they wanted to hear and the detectives were all mixed up.

Needlessly to say the jury didn't put much weight in his testimony since they unanimously convicted him of the charge of Conspiracy to Commit Murder as well as Murder. At time of sentencing he received a life sentence without the possibility of parole.

Oscar Alvarado Appeal

Alvarado contended on appeal

1. His conviction was not supported by substantial evidence
2. The trial court should have permitted him to have Pablo Alvarenga examined by a psychologist,
3. The trial court should have given a pinpoint jury instruction stating that the overt acts were not proven facts.

The appellate considered all three contentions and denied each one of them and affirmed Alvarado's conviction.

Wilson Sanchez Trial

As to Wilson's trial, it could be better described as déjà vu. All the witnesses were well experienced as to what to expect and what they would be asked in court. As to Wilson's Defense, the main hope for the Defense was trying to have his incriminating statements held inadmissible so the jury would never hear his admissions. Since the court ruled that his statements would come in, there wasn't much he could say and do. Therefore, he didn't testify like the middleman Oscar Alvarado had done. His only other Defense was to attack the testimony of his two accomplices, Erik Monroy and Pablo Alvarenga.

Needless to say, Wilson Sanchez was convicted of the Conspiracy to Commit Murder and also the Murder with the allegations of financial gain and principle armed found to be true. Likewise, he was sentenced to life without the possibility of parole.

Wilson Sanchez Appeal

When Wilson's case went up on appeal, he contended that there was insufficient corroboration of the accomplice testimony. The grounds for appeal was that the jury was improperly allowed to consider acts that occurred subsequent to the Murder as overt acts to support the conspiracy. However, the appellate court found no error and affirmed the conviction.

Witness Sally Talles

As to Sally Talles, she ended up testifying in three trials. From the beginning she was apprehensive in become involved. She wasn't the object of the crime since she was merely a bystander. She had no skin in the game but she was the one who had to lose time from work and drive all the way to the downtown courthouse at least three times. Philosophically one could say it was her civic duty to obey the subpoena requiring her to testify in court.

Thank God there are citizens like her who ultimately get involved. Initially when she talked to the police on the night of the crime, she didn't want to identify anyone since she feared that they might come after her and kill her. Even when the police asked her whether she saw the license plate number of the van she claimed she didn't see the back of the van. She thought merely giving a general description as to an old brown van with a covered window behind the driver's door wouldn't get her that involved in the case. Also pointing out where the van had been parked before the shooting couldn't be a big deal in this case. However, in the end what she saw became crucial in prosecuting the case.

Little did Sally Talles know that those two things—the description of the van and the location of the van—would be the turning points that would land five people in state prison for a long time. Although Sally most likely never thought of herself as a hero in her community, she turned out to be the type of person who makes our Criminal Justice System work. Some might say that thanks to her Justice was done.

CHAPTER 45- CRITIQUING THE INVESTIGATION

Many people in our community as well as the media enjoy criticizing law enforcement, especially detectives. These critics would say: Why didn't they do this? Why didn't they talk to that person? Why didn't they ask such and such questions? It is easy for anyone to play 'Monday Morning Quarterback.' What everyone overlooks is the fact that detectives face the situation in real time. Everything is fluid and is totally dynamic. What that means is that detectives have to make instant critical decisions without the advantage of knowing all of the facts.

Some people will claim that they have jobs in which they have to make important decisions without knowing all the facts. So, what's the big difference about detectives? The difference is that detectives have to make immediate critical decisions which can't be modified on a later date. For most people when they make the wrong initial decision, they can correct it at a later time. However, a detective who makes the wrong decision may not be able to correct it.

The reason for this is that forensic evidence at a crime scene will disappear or deteriorate if not immediately seized. The same is true with interviewing witnesses. A witness's initial statements are more reliable since their memory is better and they haven't been influenced by others as to what to say.

The Quijano case is a perfect example showing how detectives made split-second decisions which allowed them to seize crucial evidence and obtain key information from witnesses which can reveal who is the suspect(s). The Sherlock Holmes approach to solving homicide cases is based on being able to REASON BACKWARDS. In our case the shooting of the victim by the hitman was the point which the detectives have to start from.

The so-called Sherlock Homes approach to police investigation was spelled out in several books written by Sir Arthur Conan Doyle. One such book was *A Study in Scarlet* in which Sherlock Holmes explains his methodology in investigating a homicide as stated below:

"What is out of the common is usually a guide rather than a hindrance. In solving a problem of this sort, the grand thing is to be able to reason backward. That is a very useful accomplishment, and a very easy one, but people do not practice it much. In the everyday affairs of life, it is more useful to reason forwards, and so the other comes to be neglected. There are fifty who can reason synthetically for one who can reason analytically ... Most people, if you describe a train of events to them, will tell you what the result would be. They can put those events together in their minds, and argue from them that something will come to pass. There are few people however, who, if you told them a result, would be able to evolve from their own inner consciousness what the steps were which led up to that result. This power is what I mean when I talk of *reasoning backward*, or *analytically*."

What Sherlock Holmes through author Sir Arthur Conan Doyle is saying is that analytical reasoning is hard for most people. Good Detectives have that unique talent of thinking backwards. In our present case, the detectives started with finding a dead person and had to work backwards to find out who was involved with the victim's death.

Now let's review the various steps taken by the detectives in this Quijano cases immediately after finding the victim shot to death in his car.

CRIME SCENE INVESTIGATION

STEP 1 GAS BILL

ACTION-Spotting the item-The initial officer had to make a decision as to how wide of an area should be cordoned off for the CSI staff and detectives? It might seem a little extreme to include an area on the other street but it was fortuitous that the officer included such a wide area which included part of the area where the van was parked.

ACTION-Examining the item- Normally the officer coming upon a homicide crime scene would be looking for shell casings or some type of weapon. What appeared to be a piece of paper in the street would be considered trash from a litterer or something that might have been blown out of a trash truck. In this case the officer shrewdly picked up the item to examine it.

ACTION-Recognition of item- Most people would look at it but not try to figure out what it was. The officer spent the time to look over the paper and recognized that it was a utility bill from the city gas company.

ACTION-Seizing the item- Since the officer has no idea what will be relevant, the easy answer is that everything should be seized that isn't nailed down. In reality the police evidence lockers can't store so many items. Here the officer placed the gas bill back on the street so it could be collected by the CSI techs.

ACTION-Notifying others of the item- The officer was astute enough to inform his supervising sergeant of his find. Because the gas bill in the street seemed unusual enough, the officer felt it was worth mentioning.

ACTION-Detailing the location of the item- The officer was discerning enough to mention to the supervising sergeant who informed the detectives of the precise location of the gas bill.

ACTION-Understanding uniqueness of the item- The officer was sharp enough to notice that there was a name and address on the item. As a result, the item could be connected to a person who could be located.

STEP 2 EYEWITNESSES

ACTION-Who to contact? - How far from the car containing the victim should a detective go knocking on doors? Here the detectives decided to go at least three houses from the crime scene.

ACTION-When to make contact? - It was 2:00 o'clock in the morning so the issue was, should the detectives look for witnesses at that hour or wait until people are awake later in the morning? Here the detectives were perceptive enough to know that immediate contact with witnesses can be crucial.

ACTION-What questions to ask?

Question-What time did crime occur? Detectives needed to know the precise time of the shooting. Here the witnesses claim they heard shots fired around 12:10 a.m.

Question-What was heard and seen? Detectives asked Sally Talles what she heard and saw. She described hearing several gunshots and shortly thereafter saw a person running toward a van.

Question-If could identify the person? The detectives hoped that the witness could identify the shooter. Unfortunately, the witness couldn't identify any person but could say that the person appeared to be a male who was running to the van.

Question-If saw vehicle? Detectives asked about a vehicle and she told them she saw the person run to the vehicle.

Question-If saw license plate number? Detectives asked the witness if she saw or copied down the license number. She claimed that she didn't get a good look at the back of van.

Question-If vehicle was descriptive? As disappointed as the detectives were, they asked if there was anything descriptive about the vehicle. The witness said that it was old, brown utility van, and had a covering over the window behind the driver's door.

Question-Where saw vehicle? The detectives asked where the witness saw the van originally. She pointed to Arcola Avenue and indicated where she saw the van parked in the red zone.

STEP 3 CONNECTING THE ITEM (Gas Bill) TO VEHICLE

Detectives remembered what the original patrol officer had pointed out where the gas bill was found in the street on Arcola Avenue. Witness Talles pointed to same area on Arcola Avenue as the place she originally saw the van parked.

LOCATION OF ITEM (Gas Bill) SAME AS LOCATION OF VEHICLE

HYPOTHESES- Could vehicle used in committing the crime (Shooting) be at address listed on item (Gas Bill)?

Up to this point the Sherlock Holmes approach was working. Next the detectives had to test their HYPOTHESES by going to the location listed on the gas bill and looking for a distinctive brown van.

STEP 4 SURVEILLANCE OF ADDRESS ON GAS BILL

ACTION-Looking for distinctive van- Detectives went to the address on gas bill and looked for a van parked in the area. Initially the detectives didn't see any such van but later they saw a van parked on the street several houses down from the address on the gas bill. That van had a covered window next to the driver's door.

ACTION-Take photos of van- Detectives took photos of the van without being seen.

STEP 5 SHOW VEHICLE FOR IDENTIFICATION

ACTION-Show photos to eye witness- Detectives again met with the witness and showed her photos of the vans.

ACTION-Eye witness identifies vehicle- The witness told the detectives that she was certain that the photo of the old brown van was the same one she saw on the night of the shooting.

STEP 6 WHOSE VEHICLE IS IT?

ACTION-Obtain license number- Originally when the detectives spotted the van parked on the street, they copied down the license plate number.

ACTION-Determine the Registered Owner- The detectives ran the license plate number through DMV and found out that it was registered to a man who lived in South-Central LA.

ACTION-Contact RO- Detectives contacted the RO who admitted to owning the old van but had given it to his step-son to use.

ACTION-Who is step-son? - RO identifies the user of the van to be Wilson Sanchez.

STEP 7 CONNECTING DRIVER OF VEHICLE TO GAS BILL ADDRESS

ACTION-Contact Gas Bill Owner- Detectives contacted woman who lived at address and asked her about her gas bills. She indicated that her daughter had a boyfriend who lived with them by the name of Wilson Sanchez.

ACTION-Asked to explain gas bill in Sun Valley- the resident of house said that she gave her daughter the gas bill. The reason was that her daughter's boyfriend needed some form of identification to show that he lived at that address in order for him to obtain a library card.

STEP 8 WILSON SANCHEZ DROPS GAS BILL WHEN GETTING OUT OF VEHICLE

CONCLUSION- WILSON SANCHEZ WAS IN THE VICINITY OF THE SHOOTING WHEN IT OCCURRED.

CHAPTER 46 - SHERLOCK HOLMES APPROACH

The finding of the gas bill and the identification of the van were crucial in obtaining the convictions of the conspirators such as Sanchez, Alvarado, Monroy and Alvarenga. However, there wasn't sufficient evidence to obtain a conviction against the planner and brains behind the conspiracy, Maria Quijano. It was the collective effort by the detectives to obtain statements from Maria so they could prove whether she was involved and to what extent. The detectives recognized how important it was to lock Maria into a story that could be proved or disproved. These detectives were truly super sleuths in the manner they went about questioning Maria who turned out to be the ring leader of the conspirators.

Below is the methodical approach that the detectives used to elicit the incriminating statements from Maria.

STEP 1. INTERVIEW PEOPLE IN VICINITY OF SHOOTING

ACTION-House nearest to shooting- At first the police didn't know who the victim was or how he was connected to the occupants of the house next to the car where victim had been shot. After the house was connected to the victim, the detectives wanted to talk to everyone who had been inside the house.

ACTION-Interview the Next of Kin- After the victim was identified and they discovered he lived in the adjacent house, the detectives contacted the residents of that house. That was when they learned that the victim's spouse Maria Quijano lived there with the victim.

ACTION-Observe wife's reaction- Detectives were surprised that the spouse, Maria, didn't show any emotion upon hearing about her husband's death. The homicide detectives were used to spouses being distraught or hysterical upon hearing of the death of their spouse. Even though everyone expresses grief differently, the detectives were astounded at her calm demeanor.

ACTION- Listen to wife's implausible story- The detectives were good listeners to Maria's first story in which she claimed that she had been asleep and hadn't heard any shooting or anyone responding to the location.

ACTION- Asked about her cellphone- She indicated that she hadn't used her cellphone except earlier in the evening when she talked to her son about leaving his car keys at the house. The detectives obtained her cellphone number.

STEP 2 TALKED TO DAUGHTER-

ACTION-Discussion with daughter- They found out from the daughter that when she came home from work, she remembered seeing Reynaldo's Mercedes parked in front of the house. Also, she remembered hearing what she thought was Reynaldo in the adjacent bedroom. Shortly thereafter she went to sleep but was awakened by what she thought were gunshots. She remembered her mother was up and trying to quiet down the dogs.

STEP 3 OBTAIN MARIA'S CELLPHONE RECORDS

ACTION- Obtain search warrant for Maria's cellphone records- The detectives wanted to know if Maria had been asleep as she said.

ACTION- Analyzing Maria's phone records- When reviewing the phone records, the detectives notice numerous phone calls just before and after the shooting.

ACTION- Notice large number of calls to certain number- Detectives checked out that phone number and learned it was connected to Oscar Alvarado

ACTION- Obtain cellphone records on other cellphones- Detectives find that Oscar Alvarado's cellphone had contact with several other cellphones around the time of the shooting.

STEP 4 REINTERVIEW WIFE

ACTION- Asked about contacting Alvarado- The detectives asked if she knew an Oscar Alvarado and who was he. Originally, she denied knowing him.

ACTION- How much contact with Alvarado- Maria began changing her story about her contact with Alvarado.

STEP 5 CONTACTED WIFE AGAIN

ACTION- Can't explain all the calls to Alvarado-When detective asked about the 22 calls between her and Alvarado, she couldn't explain that.

ACTION-Told about location of Alvarado's cellphone- The detectives showed her a chart/map which showed that Alvarado's cellphone was near her house at the time of the shooting. She couldn't explain how that could happen.

ACTION- Use Ruse technique- The detectives gave her a soft landing by alluding to the fact that no one could blame her for what she did to a no-good cheating husband. Then she stated that she was in contact with Oscar Alvarado to find someone to beat up her husband. Then she explained that the other guys went too far. When asked whether she knew that the beating could result in his death she said she realized that was a possibility.

CONCLUSION- MARIA ADMITTED THAT THE NATURAL PROBABLE CONSEQUENCE COULD BE DEATH.

By having the LAPD Homicide Detectives from North Hollywood Division using the so call Sherlock Holmes approach all of the conspirators were convicted in one way or the other. Years ago, Sir Arthur Conan Doyle had a

magnificent way of expressing what made for an exceptional detective. His approach was spelled out in many of his books and is a brilliant way to investigate a Murder case. It was explained as follows:

In order to solve a puzzle, you need to know exactly what the puzzle is. Sherlock Holmes' approach to solving a crime started by defining the great mystery of a case. He took all the available data he had obtained and created a comprehensive portrait that consisted of what he knew, the facts, observations, as well as answers to questions asked. Then analyze all this data, and create a hypothesis. This approach allowed him to better focus on the facts that mattered.

Good detectives rely on Holmes' approach to solving complex cases. They use the same meticulous approach and often the detective will list all the facts on a board. In this way the detective can see every item pertaining to the crime. However, he will highlight the relevant facts while the irrelevant facts still remain, however, they fade into the background. Real detectives can easily see which salient points they need to concentrate on and expend their energy on.

Whenever Holmes started a case, he approached it with an open mind, with absolutely no presumptions formed. Everyone was a suspect. Holmes believed that a detective shouldn't have preconceived ideas of what happened. Instead of guessing first, it is important to work with the information you have and then try to develop a reasonable solution. Whatever you discover, however illogical it may be, you will be on your way to finding the truth.

In order to understand the story behind each Murder, you must be able to interpret the narrative correctly. Develop your detective skills by taking the time to examine each area you pursue. Holmes was brilliant at that. He would assess the situation and make observations of everything around him. At that point Holmes would create a narrative that explained what actually happened.

Holmes like any good detective knew the importance of any scenario must be supported by logic. In order to solve a crime, the detective like Holmes needs to know how to sift through the facts to see the logical connections pointing to the suspects.

Holmes prided himself in having a good understanding of people's actions and habits. He believed in order to be perceptive one has to be a listener. It is important that a detective listen to all parties. By mixing with people you learn more about them and may pick up clues. The best way to encourage people to talk is to be polite to them. When they start speaking, remain silent. The ability to be a good listener often catches liars. Those who are telling stories find it harder to keep the facts straight.

To Holmes everyone was capable of committing a Murder. It was only a question of unraveling the mystery behind 'How.' A detective must never underestimate the people he is dealing with. People commit crimes for different motives. Sometimes it is uncontrolled passion, ruthless planning, or a combination of both. Holmes recognized that people were driven by complex emotions, and therefore capable of committing the worst crime under certain conditions. Holmes recognized that just because someone didn't fit the usual stereotype wasn't a reason to reject them as a suspect. Holmes' motto was, "Consider everything."

Holmes understood that in every investigation the detective comes across dozens and dozens of facts. The discerning detective can analyze all these facts and determine which ones are vital and which ones are incidental. Often a Murder is solved by only several facts. Knowing how to spot this is the first step to becoming a super sleuth detective.

Having a keen eye for detail and strong analytic skills is the key to becoming a good detective. You need to work with the right strategy. Holmes placed a high emphasis on collecting, analyzing, and deducing from information. It is important to gather as much evidence and data as possible. Whatever deductions Holmes made, he did it based on the evidence found. As Sherlock pointed out, "It is a capital mistake to theorize before you have all the evidence. It biases the judgment. Don't just guess. Investigate."

That is why Sherlock Holmes or at least Sir Arthur Conan Doyle would have been pleased with the investigative skills exhibited by these LAPD detectives. THEIR DILIGENCE AND THEIR ABILITY TO REASON BACKWARDS SNARED THESE FIVE CONSPIRATORS INVOLVED IN MURDER.

Made in United States
North Haven, CT
04 November 2026

21770333R00166